FROM HOLLOW TO HOPEFUL

NAVIGATING THE GRIEF OF MISCARRIAGE AND INFANT LOSS

CHERI Y. HALVORSON

Visit the author online at MerryHeartMinistries.net

Merry Heart Ministries, LLC

From Hollow to Hopeful: Navigating the Grief of Miscarriage and Infant Loss

Copyright © 2026 by Cheri Y. Halvorson. All rights reserved.

Cover art by Hannah Linder Designs.

Edited by Blair Parke.

All Scripture references, unless otherwise indicated, are from the *The New Scofield Study Bible, New King James Version* (NKJV). Edited by C. I. Scofield. Thomas Nelson Publishers, 1989.

Other citations of scripture include the following translations of the Bible (scripture access available via Biblegateway.com/versions):

Amplified (AMP), Christian Standard Bible (CSB), English Standard Version (ESV), New International Version (NIV), New Living Translation (NLT), and New American Standard Bible (NASB).

Contents

Introduction   VII

Part 1:

Acknowledging Baby's Life and Loss

    1.   Recognizing Baby's Life and Humanness   3

    2.   Acknowledging and Honoring Baby's Passing   11

    3.   When Others Don't (or Won't) Acknowledge Baby's Loss   27

Part 2:

Lamenting Baby's Loss

    4.   Cry out to the Lord   43

    5.   Complain to and Question the Lord   55

    6.   Request of the Lord   69

    7.   Turning Point: Remember the Lord   81

    8.   Praise the Lord   97

    9.   The Impacts of Praise   109

Part 3:

Life After Loss

10. Weep with Those Who Weep 125

11. Turning Your Trials into Trails 135

12. Moving Forward: Living with Scars and Hope 151

Acknowledgments 163

Appendix A:
The Prevalence of Miscarriage and Infant Loss 165

Appendix B:
Miscarriage and Infant Loss Survey 169

Appendix C:
Medical Terminology for Babies, Miscarriage, and Infant Loss ... 175

Appendix D:
Psalms of Lamentation 177

Appendix E:
The Gospel in a Nutshell 181

Appendix F:
The Names of God and Their Meanings 185

Appendix G:
Hebrew and Greek Words Translated as "Praise" 187

Appendix H:
A Deeper Dive into Praise 191

Appendix I:
"Great Is Thy Faithfulness" Lyrics 199

Appendix J:
CCRRE Template for Mourning 201

Bibliography 203

About the Author 213

Introduction

The shaft of pain that shoots from gut to heart, the soundless cry
that shakes the body and wrenches the soul, the groaning that
emanates from deep within, the hot tears that stream down cheeks
until it seems there are no more left to flow,
the sense of emptiness and loss—
unspeakable, agonizing loss:
This is grief.

"Oh, Sissy," I sighed. "I'm so, so sorry!"

The knuckles of my hand went white as I pressed the phone closer to my ear. My daughter's first child—my first grandchild—had been miscarried at nine weeks' gestation.

The thousand miles between us suddenly felt like a million. I was not there to take my daughter in my arms and hold her, cry with her, grieve with her. All moisture seemed to have evaporated from my mouth, but I forced a swallow and managed to whisper, "I know how painful this is. I can't tell you that the pain will go away because the pain never really goes away. It just gets easier to bear."

As I later reflected upon this feeble attempt at consolation, the muscles in my lower abdomen tightened involuntarily. There it was again—that old, familiar pain. The pain of broken dreams. The pain of unanswered questions. The pain of the awareness of absent children—children I would never get to see this side of heaven except in fuzzy, black-and-white ultrasound images.

Lying on a gurney with a gel-covered belly, I am in the nineteenth week of pregnancy with my third child. I glance over at my husband, Eric, who sits by my side, and as I prop up my head on my arm for a better view of the ultrasound screen, we prepare to get our first glimpse of Baby. White "snow" drifts against a black background, initially obscuring our view of anything remotely resembling a human being when suddenly, the bones of Baby's face appear, and in the chest cavity just below, a tiny heart flutters. Soon afterward, two small hands begin to wave until a thumb manages to find its way into Baby's mouth. The technician moves the ultrasound wand and takes measurements of Baby's skull, heart, stomach, legs, and spine. Minutes later, we get another frontal view of Baby's face, the jaw opening and closing as if mouthing an inaudible message. Gazing at the little face on the screen, I smile and turn my head to look at Eric, who grins in reply.

The technician taps her keyboard to freeze the frame and types across the screen, "Bye for now." The screen goes black while the VCR below the monitor whirs, shooting its tape tray forward, and as the technician removes the video-tape and hands it to me, she has no way of recognizing the precious gift she is presenting to my husband and me.

Although our bookcase shelves are lined with dozens of photo albums that chronicle the lives of our four children who were delivered full-term, that video-tape contains the only images preserved of our third baby who would pass away *in utero* one week later.[1]

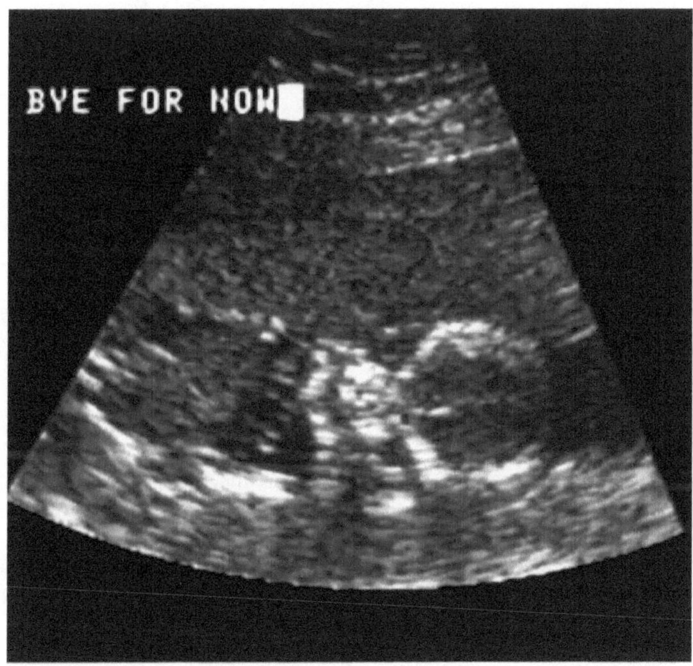

FIGURE 1. *Ultrasound Image of Baby at Nineteen Weeks' Gestation*

Tears burned my eyes as scorching questions erupted from my mouth.

"'The pain just gets easier to bear with time?' Really? Are these the best words of condolence I have to offer a grieving mother?"

With a blinding flash, reality dawned upon me: I was still grieving the babies I had lost during my third and fourth pregnancies! Time had not made much of an impact on my sense of loss, for the pain was still there—maybe not as fresh and debilitating as at first, but when the waves of sorrow came, they were nearly as gut-wrenching decades later as they were the days they happened. How was this possible? Much like a cancer that I thought was in remission, grief recurred unbidden and unexpectedly again and again, eating away at my heart.

There has to be a better way of processing the deaths of my unborn children than this grit-my-teeth-and-suffer-through-the-heartache technique I've been using for nearly three decades, I told myself. *I don't just need to find a new method for grieving. I need to find* God's *method for grieving—both for my own sake and for every other mother I encounter who is going through the heartache of the loss of a baby.*

There are a lot of us out there—far too many in the United States (US) and around the world who have endured perinatal loss[2]—and you, dear sister, may be one in need of the Lord's guidance and comfort in mourning the passing of your baby. (Appendix A provides a glimpse of the prevalence of miscarriage and stillbirth in developed countries.) For these reasons, I have compiled within these pages insights from my interviews with fifteen parents[3] who lost babies at different stages of pregnancy and post-pregnancy, and I've also included information on perinatal loss and grief from medical and psychological studies. (See Appendix B for the grief survey completed by interviewees.)

However, I want you to understand that the book before you now is not intended to be a self-help manual with the promise of a shortcut to the proverbial light at the end of the tunnel; neither is this book intended to help you "come to terms with" or find relief from your grief. No, relief is temporary. What you require is hope in your Heavenly Father and in His ability to *restore* you.

I don't mean the kind of restoration that was required in the Old Testament when an item or animal was lost or stolen.[4] I'm talking about the kind of restoration that David describes in the 23rd Psalm:

> The Lord is my shepherd; I shall not want.
> He makes me to lie down in green pastures;
> He leads me beside the still waters.
> He restores [*shûwb*] my soul.[5]

You see, the Good Shepherd's restoration is not wishful thinking that the Lord will take you back to the way things were before your loss. The Lord's restoration is all-encompassing: It's a rescue, a retrieval, and a refreshing of your soul. It's a recovery from and a reversal of a life of pain.

You may not have thought this kind of restoration possible, but since the Lord has provided for His children in every other area of our lives, there should be no doubt that Our Heavenly Father has also made a way to navigate loss. This method is called *lamentation*, and it provides a kind of comfort that is more complete than anything the world has to offer. I know this to be true, for I have experienced the goodness, grace, and mercy of the Lord myself as I lamented the loss of two of my babies.

Dear sister, my prayer for you is that by putting into practice God's plan for mourning, you will understand what it means to have *hope* in the Lord. You'll have confidence in Him, trust in Him, and take your refuge in Him not only while you are in mourning but in all areas of your life.[6]

---

1. *Merriam-Webster Dictionary Online*, "In *utero*: in the uterus; before birth," last updated December 13, 2025, https://www.merriam-webster.com/dictionary/in%2 0utero.

2. Cassidy, "The Disenfranchisement of Perinatal Grief," 710. *Perinatal grief* is defined as "the experience of loss following the death of a baby at any time during pregnancy (miscarriage, stillbirth, termination of pregnancy for medical reasons) or in the neonatal period."

3. Fourteen mothers and one father (none of whom were married to one another) completed my 55-question survey on perinatal loss and grief (see Appendix B). Combined, these parents lost 24 babies: 11 were 6–12 weeks' gestation; 10 were 14–22 weeks' gestation; 2 were 24–27+ weeks' gestation; and one baby passed away three months after full-term delivery.

4. Strong, *Strong's Exhaustive Concordance*, under "H7999, *shâlam*: to restore, repay, recompense, make restitution."

5. Strong, *Strong's Exhaustive Concordance*, under "(H7725), *shûwb*: to turn back (not necessarily with the idea of return to the starting point); to recompense, recover, refresh, relieve, requite, rescue, restore, retrieve, reverse, reward."

6. Strong, *Strong's Exhaustive Concordance*, under "H4009, *mibtach*: a refuge, hope, cofidence, and trust"; and under "H4268, *machaseh* or *machseh*: hope, (place of) refuge, shelter, trust."

Part 1:

Acknowledging Baby's Life and Loss

MERRY HEART MINISTRIES

CHAPTER ONE

Recognizing Baby's Life and Humanness

Oh, send out Your light and Your truth!
Let them lead me.
PSALM 43:3

ONE BRISK, WINTER MORNING, I marched into the living room with a dust rag in one hand, a spray-bottle of orange furniture polish under my arm, and a flurry of ideas swirling in my head for how to proceed with this book. Now, I'm no Martha Stewart, but it hadn't been very long since I had last dusted the furniture, so I wasn't expecting this to be an all-day project. However, as the early morning sun peeked through the adjacent window, a shudder of horror coursed through my body. Suddenly visible were millions, nay, gazillions of glittering flecks of dust, dancing on the rays of sunshine between me and the television, and on the console before me were strands of hair, dust bunnies, and substances-of-unknown-origin that I hadn't noticed before.

"What...? How...? Where did all this dust come from?" I screeched to no one else in the room. "This is disgusting! How did I not see this before?"

Snatching the furniture polish from beneath my arm, I sprayed down the console and nearby coffee table. As I swirled the dust rag with slightly more fury than necessary, the Lord gave me a revelation in answer to my questions: "The dust was there, but you couldn't see it because you hadn't shined enough light on it."

My Heavenly Father's words immediately reminded me of one of my dear ol' dad's frequently used expressions. Nearly every time he switched on the lights in our home, he'd say, "Let's shed a little light on the subject." We kids were often so engrossed in playing a game, watching TV, or doing homework that we had failed to notice the gradual dimming of the light in the room as the sun went down. In other words, we had gotten so accustomed to the semi-darkness that we didn't appreciate how poor our perspective had become until Dad turned on the light.

You're very good at the object lessons, Lord, I thought as I stared down at the dust bunnies that seemed to have multiplied exponentially in the last few seconds and were hopping freely about my living room. *I get it. You're not criticizing my housekeeping skills—You're showing me what happens when I rely solely upon my own perspective of things. I thought there was a minor need here, and you exposed the reality of a problem I didn't even know existed.*

The truth of the matter is that some parents view infant loss through the lens of their own understanding or that of their medical providers without taking into account the Lord's perspective of life within the womb. Consider what might be exposed by shining the light of God's Word on the circumstances of your pregnancy and loss. Viewing that tiny life from the Lord's perspective will allow you to see your circumstances with a clarity unavailable to your own eyes. With clarity comes understanding, with understanding comes wisdom, and "wisdom," as the Lord has informed us, "is the principal thing."[1]

Yes, the Lord has blessed human beings with intelligence and inventiveness, but the Bible tells us that our wisdom (or our ways) are not God's ways, and our thoughts are not God's thoughts.[2] If you, dear sister, will recognize these three things, your journey of grief will begin on the right course:

1. God sees all aspects of any circumstance, including those things of which we are not even aware.

2. He knows best how to handle each circumstance.

3. He knows best what we need and how and when to meet these needs.[3]

Do not think for an instant that I am implying that the Lord caused the loss of your child to "teach you something." This is a lie from the pit of hell, and don't let anyone try to tell you otherwise! I am saying that when you recognize God's sovereignty and His wisdom, you can confidently rely upon Him for comfort and for guidance in how to view the life that was in your womb and how to proceed with mourning the loss of this life.

Bringing Baby's Life into the Light

Grief can be a tricky thing that catches you off-guard. Just when you think you have a handle on your emotions, an invitation to a baby shower arrives in the mail. Someone who doesn't know about your loss asks about your pregnancy. The smell of antiseptic triggers a memory of your hospital experience. Circumstances such as these sometimes feel like a lightning bolt striking a power pole: In a flash, you are shocked back into the darkness of sorrow.

As you sit there in the shadows, I know that you have great need of some light—even more than truth and enlightenment, you need the presence of God, for your Heavenly Father is indeed light, and only His light can drive away the darkness that enfolds you. This isn't hyperbole. Consider what the disciple John records of Jesus:

- "I am the light of the world."[4]

- "I have come as a light into the world, that whoever believes in Me should not abide in darkness."[5]

- "In Him was life, and that life was the light of all mankind. The light shines in the darkness, and the darkness has not overcome it."[6]

Have confidence in the fact that, as the author and source of light, the Lord's presence conquers all forms of darkness, including the darkness of *physical death*.

Let's again turn to the Word of God for proof of this truth. Zacharias, the father of John the Baptist, prophesied that the Messiah was coming "to give light to those who sit in darkness and the shadow of death, to guide our feet into the way of peace."[7] In addition to revealing the Messiah's primary goal of redeeming humans from the sin that separates them from God, Zacharias's words also explain that Jesus (our Messiah) *illuminates the path to peace for those who sit in the shadow of grief cast by death.*

Jesus Himself made this promise as well during His Sermon on the Mount: "Blessed are those who mourn, for they shall be comforted."[8] This means that all those who come to Him with their sorrow will be divinely favored and provided with the tools to process their grief. As a result of this blessing, they will obtain comfort—true comfort that only the Lord can bestow.

Dear sister, understand that your pain is not invisible to the Lord: He sees every shattered piece of your broken heart, and only He is capable of mending each fragment. One of the mothers I interviewed for this book who lost three children to miscarriage described the effects of God's love and light on the darkness of her sorrow:

> It's as if the cuts of pain dig a furrow into the soil of our hearts
> that only hold shadows and the cool, dark of something only
> you feel. And yet the eyes of the Lord are even in the deep, and

the night is as day to Him. It's as if the trenches and cuts in their hollowness create a space where only the hand of God can pour out His Spirit and reach to all the depths and touch each broken piece of soil.

The Lord sees all the recesses, all the nooks and crannies where pain tries to hide, and God your Healer is the only one who can illuminate these shadowy areas and fill them with His love and comfort.

Acknowledging Baby's Humanness

Understanding one important truth about your pregnancy from the outset will make all the difference in advancing the grieving process for the loss of your baby. Your pregnancy wasn't just a clump of cells. From the moment of conception, you were pregnant with a human being—one who is precious to your Heavenly Father and one who is known by Him, planned by Him, and designed by Him.

This is why you are grieving after your miscarriage or stillbirth right now. Your spirit recognizes that your miscarriage was not merely an unfortunate medical event. You lost a *child*.

Let the Word of God shine His light on the fact of your child's humanness. The master psalmist, King David, makes it clear that within his mother's womb, God orchestrated his creation and design:

> For You formed my inward parts;
> You covered me in my mother's womb.
> I will praise You, for I am fearfully [*yârê'*] and wonderfully
> [*pâlâh*] made;
> Marvelous [*pâlâ'*] are Your works,
> And that my soul knows very well.
> My frame was not hidden from You,
> When I was made in secret,

And skillfully wrought in the lowest parts of the earth.
Your eyes saw my substance, being yet unformed.
And in Your book, they all were written,
The days fashioned for me,
When as yet there were none of them.[9]

David is in a state of wonder, marveling at his creation, and there is no question in his mind that God's hand was responsible for this miracle. David recognizes that he was indeed "David" before his body was even formed—when the only eyes that could see him belonged to the Lord. More than this, David also acknowledges that God had a plan for his life long before it began.

The prophets Isaiah and Jeremiah also emphasize the status of unborn children by explaining how Yahweh knows people as human beings while they are still developing within their mothers. Think about how the following verses, although specific to the prophets themselves, extend to every human being:

- "Thus says the Lord, your Redeemer, / And He who formed Me from the womb: / 'I am the Lord, who makes all things.'"[10]

- "Thus says the Lord who made you and formed you from the womb, who will help you: 'Fear not, O Jacob My servant; And you, Jeshurun, whom I have chosen.'"[11]

- "Before I formed you in the womb I knew you;
  Before you were born, I set you apart;
  I appointed you as a prophet to the nations."[12]

This last scripture from Jeremiah reveals that the Lord not only knew each one of us as a human being prior to our birth, but our omniscient Father also knew and planned the reason for our existence well before we were created: "In the foreknowledge of God we each, like Jeremiah, have—from eternity—an identity and purpose in the Creator's mind."[13]

The Bible makes it clear that God designs, plans, and knows His children as human beings before they are in their mothers' womb—and this includes *your* baby.

I therefore encourage you, dear sister, go to your Heavenly Father and allow the light of His Word to comfort you as He reveals the truth of your baby's existence and humanness. When you bring the life of your baby into the Lord's light—light that illuminates the hidden, unknown things—your healing process may begin.

---

1. Prov. 4:7.

2. Isa. 55:8.

3. Heb. 4:13; Ps. 33:13–15; Prov. 5:21; Prov. 19:21; Ps. 139:1–4; Rom. 8:28; Jer. 29:11; Isa. 55:8-9.

4. John 8:12.

5. John 12:46.

6. John 1:4–5, NIV.

7. Luke 1:79.

8. Matt. 5:4. Strong, *Strong's Exhaustive Concordance*, under "G3107, *makariŏs*: supremely blessed, fortunate, well off."

9. Ps. 139:13–16. Strong, *Strong's Exhaustive Concordance*, under "H3372, *yârê*: to revere"; "H6395, *pâlâh*: to distinguish, separate, make wonderfully"; "H6381, *pâlâ*: distinguish, to make great, marvelous."

10. Isa. 49:5.

11. Isa. 44:2. *Jeshurun* means "the upright one," and refers to Israel.

12. Jer. 1:5, NIV.

13. Ling, *When Does Human Life Begin?*, 10.

CHAPTER TWO

Acknowledging and Honoring Baby's Passing

The Lord is close to the brokenhearted
and saves those who are crushed in spirit.
PSALM 34:18, NIV

STRETCHED OUT ON A gurney, I winced as the technician squirted over my bare belly ultrasound gel that had evidently been stored in the dark recesses of an arctic cave. My obstetrician (OB) had sent me from her office to an ultrasound facility to get more advanced imaging following my twenty-week checkup because the baby was measuring smaller than expected.

After her initial greetings to Eric and me, the tech remained unusually quiet throughout the ultrasound. No friendly chatter or small talk was exchanged as she rolled the imaging wand over my abdomen, pausing occasionally to tap on the keyboard. About five minutes later, and with few words to either of us, the tech excused herself to get a doctor.

The physician greeted us with even fewer words, quickly took his place on the rolling chair near the monitor, grabbed the ultrasound wand, and began to scan my uterus.

"Have you had any cramping recently?" he asked, keeping his eyes glued to the imaging screen.

"No." My answer was quick and emphatic.

"Have you had any bleeding recently?" he continued.

Startled, I hesitated this time before answering, "No." This line of questioning didn't bode well.

Dragging my eyes away from the doctor's dark expression, I craned my neck to see the image of my baby on the monitor over my right shoulder. As the sound of blood thudded in my ears, my eyes bored into the imaging screen, straining to see movement from Baby—*any* kind of movement—especially in Baby's chest cavity.

"There is very little amniotic fluid," the doctor stated flatly.

I frantically scanned every square millimeter of the monitor and began to pray silently. *Please, God! Please replace the amnionic fluid!*

Illogical as it may seem, I thought that if I prayed hard enough and stared long enough, the fluid would suddenly appear. Then the doctor would be able to see my baby better. Then he would find the baby's heartbeat. Then he would tell me everything was okay and that his concerns were just a mistake.

"We're not seeing any movement here," the doctor said, finally turning toward me. "We can't find a heartbeat, and we've been looking for a long time." Although spoken softly, the doctor's words sliced through the chaos of my thoughts like a scalpel.

"So you're saying the baby isn't alive?" Eric's voice reverberated through the stillness of the room despite being uttered just above a whisper.

He had the strength to ask what I refused to express for fear of making the words fact.

My breath caught in my chest as I desperately searched the screen before the doctor replied, "Yes, that's what I am saying."

This can't be true! I screamed inside my head. *No, you are wrong! My baby is right there! I can see the little body plain as day!*

Gravely, the doctor informed me that I needed to see my OB. He then told me he was sorry and slowly escorted us from the room.

Back in the car, I cradled my belly with both hands, pleading for my baby to move. Maybe the doctors were wrong. After all, it hadn't been that long since I'd felt the baby kick, right? Wasn't it just yesterday?

"Move, baby, move!" I sobbed. "I know you are in there. You can't be gone!"

I just couldn't bring myself to say that my baby had died—the words simply refused to form in my mouth. This new reality didn't seem *real*. The loss had been so sudden, and there had been no warning or indication of Baby's passing. No blood. No pain. Nothing made sense. It was too hard to acknowledge that my baby's life was at an end—that the hopes and plans Eric and I had had for this baby were at an end...

Overcoming Denial

I was in denial about Baby's passing. I had erected a bulwark to defend my heart from the tidal wave of pain that had crashed over me, and you, dear sister, may also have built a barrier around your heart and mind as a means of protection from sorrow.

Denial is a refusal to believe the truth of a matter, and although it is a common coping mechanism, denial is complex and comes in many forms. For example, denial may be an involuntary response—a means of cushioning the blow of the painful experience of infant loss, allowing parents time to adjust to a changing situation.[1] Denial might (as in my case) be an initial inability to accept a doctor's diagnosis of Baby's passing, or it could be a firm belief that it's all a huge mistake.

Denial may also be a conscious attempt to avoid acknowledging the humanity of the pregnancy. You see, if parents convince themselves that it was "merely a mass of tissue" developing within the womb, it is easier to believe there was no life lost, and if there was no loss, there is nothing to grieve, and if there is nothing to grieve, life can go on as usual.[2]

No matter the reasons for denial, know that the only way to overcome a false belief is with truth—the truth that you were pregnant with a human being and the truth that you also experienced the loss of that precious life.

If you have not already done so, say this aloud: *"My baby died."*

I understand that the brevity of these words is not equal to their weight. In fact, expressing them may be one of the hardest things you'll ever do, but say these words you must.

Grief often holds a heart captive, but remember, the Lord promised that the truth is the key to freedom. Jesus said, "If you abide in My word, you are My disciples indeed. And you shall know the truth, and the truth shall make you free."[3] Do not let your familiarity with this scripture undermine its significance, especially regarding your baby's life and death. If Jesus said His truth is freeing, it is essential for you to look to His Word to discover the truth: the truth of the life and humanity of your Baby, the truth of Baby's death, and the truth of your grief.

Acknowledging and declaring your loss aloud is an expression of truth that begins the process of unburdening your heart of heaviness and helping you to find solace in your sorrow.

Taking Time to Grieve

"Time heals all wounds." "Time is a great healer." "Give it Time."

Oh, the clichés offered to those in mourning.

I got *so* tired of hearing how time was going to aid my grieving process because time seemed more like my enemy than a cure. I felt betrayed by time and its promises of relief because my pain didn't seem to lessen as each page of the calendar was turned. The responsibilities of life kept me busy and moving, but the tendrils of grief rooted their way deep into my inner being, and every now and again, a fresh shoot of sorrow would break through the crusty shell I'd carefully packed around my heart as an act of self-preservation.

What was my problem? Why was I still so sad and disappointed months—even years—after the fact, despite the many blessings in my life? Why couldn't I shake this?

Short answer: I hadn't allowed myself time to properly grieve.

Giving ourselves permission to grieve perinatal loss in the same way we would grieve any other loss is essential, but unfortunately, parents are not always intentional about making time to mourn. When asked what advice they wished to give others who have lost children, 73.3% of parents I interviewed directly expressed the importance of setting aside time to grieve perinatal loss. One mother stressed, "Give yourself the time and space to be sad. Then move forward, if only one step at a time." Learn from the experience of others who have traveled a similar road. When they say you need to give yourself the opportunity to grieve, do so.

My mother-in-law, Lennie, was one who emphasized to me the value of intentionally taking time to grieve. After her three-month old daughter died of pneumonia (a complication of the cystic fibrosis that had gone undiagnosed until shortly before Baby passed), time for grieving was a luxury Lennie didn't believe she could afford because she still had three other children and a household to care for. A few months later, she was feeling tired, rundown, and irritable, so she went to see her general practitioner.

The doctor examined her and then asked, "Have you cried over your baby?" When Lennie explained that she hadn't had time to cry, he told her sternly, "Go home and cry. You need to have a good cry."

Nearly sixty years after the fact, Lennie vividly remembers this admonishment and makes the same recommendation to other grieving parents, reminding them that they should not feel guilty about mourning their loss.

Another thing to keep in mind is that there truly is no such thing as a typical amount of time for your period of mourning. Grief is a complex, time-consuming process:

> [T]here seems to be an interminability to grief. Grief often does not keep to a schedule. It is a timeless, nonlinear procession of emotions that rises and falls. The reality of the child's death includes the grief over the possibilities and potential loss, the endless wondering over what it would be like if the baby were still alive day-by-day.[4]

Mourning the loss of your child and the life you would have had with that child truly requires *time*. In fact, research has shown that the most emotional period for parents is between three months and two years after the loss, but "it may take up to seven years to recover from the death of a child."[5] One reason for this is that parents who experience infant loss—including early pregnancy and ectopic pregnancy losses—are at high risk for PTSD, depression, and anxiety.[6] Thus, the process of grief is more serious and complicated than many realize and should not be rushed. Your mourning period will take as long as it takes.

It is also important to remember mothers typically require more time to cope with perinatal loss than friends and other family members, including babies' fathers. One mother explained to me that most people in her life were "able to close the chapter and move on" much quicker than she could and that "it seemed to be easier for [her husband] and others" to cope with their grief than it was for her. Another mother I interviewed advised, "It's ok to grieve as you need to. Take your time and don't allow others to make you feel like you need to move on. We all feel emotional things differently."

The sad truth is, other people *will* move on from your loss faster than you will because they are not living with the loss day to day. Give yourself some grace, allow yourself to grieve, and take as much time as you need.

Ways to Openly Acknowledge Baby's Loss

With the blue glow of a computer monitor reflecting off my glasses, I eagerly opened an email from one of the mothers I'd interviewed regarding her experiences with miscarriage. My forefinger stopped scrolling and froze in mid-air over the computer mouse when I came upon the following statement:

> My husband and I had not told many people about the pregnancy, and I found that it was difficult to process what I felt was a "hidden loss."

Hidden loss. The words leapt off the screen and ricocheted around my brain. This mother's characterization of the veiled nature of her grief echoed terms recently coined by researchers in the stacks of medical and psychological studies I'd been gathering: "ambiguous loss" and "invisible death."[7] Scholars use these phrases to describe the *vagueness* associated with deaths of babies in utero, the *ambiguity* created by unanswerable questions and differing perceptions of early pregnancy, the *invisibility* of a pregnancy lost before it was obvious to the world, and the *lack of acknowledgment* of the loss of a child for whom there was no burial or memorial.

This hidden quality of miscarriage is often what makes it so difficult for many parents to properly mourn their babies. The death of a child before he or she is born—especially one who was unseen outside the womb even by the mother herself—commonly goes unacknowledged and unmarked by those outside of the immediate family.[8] Bereavement specialist Sandra Howlett emphasized parents' yearning for public recognition of their children: "What a bereaved parent needs to hear is that their child's life mattered, however short it was, and that the little one will be remembered."[9] It is for this very reason that, in addition to acknowledging your loss verbally, you should also commemorate your child's passing in a tangible manner and with other people present.[10]

The desire to honor their babies' memories was expressed by most of the parents I interviewed for this book as well. One mother explained, "No one way to grieve is right or wrong. Not everyone is going to feel the same loss or the same emotions, [so] find something that helps you remember that baby as often or as little as you want." Yet another mother stressed the necessity of grieving as you see fit because there is "no one-size-fits-all" method of mourning.

What matters is that you do something that is special, significant to you, and outwardly acknowledges your baby's loss.

The various ways in which the parents I interviewed grieved and memorialized their children included memorial services, saving mementos, infant loss remembrance activities, and naming the babies who had passed. The following explanations of each of these methods are provided as an encouragement for you to find ways to include family and friends in honoring your child.

Funerals and Memorial Services

In the West, a funeral is typically held to honor the memory and celebrate the life of someone who has passed away, but funerals are not simply for the deceased; these services also provide a socially approved means for family and friends to openly grieve loss.[11] A funeral is an indication to the world that the person who was lost will be missed and is worthy of being mourned.

However, Western culture offers no comparable rituals for commemorating miscarriage, and the unfortunate effect of this is that the grieving process for this kind of loss may become repressed or prolonged.[12] Scholars of perinatal grief explained that the absence of "commemorative activities...made [grieving parents] feel deprived of the right to mourn, which increased their distress and suffering."[13] I found this to be the case for my own miscarriages as well as for those of the parents I interviewed: Out of twenty-three babies lost, only four were memorialized with funerals, meaning the majority of parents were forced to grieve their losses in solitude and without the physical and emotional support of others.

Consider the problems created by the failure to formally address a baby's passing: When there is no body to bury, there is typically no funeral, no memorial, no monument. Even more significantly, there is no grave for parents to visit, no headstone to adorn with flowers, and seemingly, no evidence left on earth of the precious, little life. This lack of acknowledgement is often difficult for parents to bear.

It's time to flip the script. Don't worry if no one else in your family has ever held a service after a miscarriage; the benefits of honoring the life of your child outweigh what others think. It also doesn't matter how long it has been since Baby passed; commemorating the life of your child and performing a remembrance ritual or ceremony is a meaningful way of coping with your loss.

Therefore, I encourage you to invite immediate family members and/or close friends to acknowledge the loss of your miscarried child as a death—a death as significant as any other—with a funeral or memorial of some kind. Hold a remembrance service. Plant a tree or special flowers. Play music. Release balloons. Make it personal and make it special. Baby's memory deserves to be honored, and your heart needs the freedom to express the fullness of your grief and your love.

Mementos

Although the majority of the parents I interviewed did not have formal memorial services for their children, 67% of parents saved mementos which continue to hold special places in their hearts. Keepsakes and rituals are especially important coping mechanisms for parents in the first two years after loss "when social support decreases."[14] Mementos validate parenthood, but even more than this, they provide tangible evidence of a baby's brief life long after others have forgotten about Baby's existence.[15]

My own mementos are precious reminders of my absent children. I marked the babies' due dates with journal entries to preserve their memories. I have a necklace of six figures with birthstones at their center, and the figures representing my two children in heaven are differentiated by their tiny wings. I also bought a special porcelain doll to honor the memory of my third baby. I confess that initially, whenever I saw the doll, I felt the pang of loss, but with the passage of time, the doll became a sweet reminder of the child whose home is in heaven.

Mementos are as personal and individual as each person, so I recommend you select something meaningful to you, even if you are the only one who knows its significance. Here are a few examples of the remembrances cherished by parents I interviewed:

- Sonograms

- Plants and silk flowers
  (These gifts are decades old and are still displayed within view of each mother.)

- Memory boxes to hold hospital bracelets, pictures, handprints or footprints, and locks of hair

- A handmade quilt, stamped with Baby's footprints

- Necklaces with angel wings or Baby's name

- Stuffed animals

- Christmas stockings and ornaments

- Tattoos of Baby's name or footprints

- Photos of Baby and/or family
  (Some photos were taken by professionals, and others were posted on social media to announce Baby's birth and passing.)

- Journals dedicated to saving a record of the experience of Baby's passing, the mother's feelings of grief, and/or letters to Baby

Pregnancy and Infant Loss Remembrance

During the late twentieth century, awareness of the significance of infant loss began to rise. In 1988, President Ronald Reagan designated the month of October as Pregnancy and Infant Loss Awareness Month and issued the following Presidential Proclamation:

National observance of Pregnancy and Infant Loss Awareness Month, 1988, offers us the opportunity to increase our understanding of the great tragedy involved in the deaths of unborn and newborn babies. It also enables us to consider how, as individuals and communities, we can meet the needs of bereaved parents and family members and work to prevent causes of these problems."[16]

Observance of infant loss has since spread across the globe. To raise awareness of SIDS,[17] miscarriage, stillbirth, and newborn mortality in the US, a group led by Robyn Baer petitioned the House of Representatives in 2006 to mark October 15 as World Pregnancy and Infant Loss Remembrance Day—a day now also commemorated in the UK, Canada, and Australia. At 7:00 p.m. in all four countries, a special observance is held: "In all time zones, candles are lit and kept burning for one hour, creating a 24-hour 'wave of light' as it moves around the world in reverence of beloved babies who are dearly loved and forever missed."[18] In addition, cities around the world host remembrance walks every October to honor the memories of those lost far too young.

I encourage you to find a way to participate in Infant Loss Awareness Month to honor your baby's passing. Wear commemorative jewelry (many options are available through various organizations and companies online), post a reminder on social media, or join a remembrance walk event. Much like a support group, these gatherings and outreaches will give you an opportunity to meet other parents who have traveled a similar path of grief. Each of the parents I interviewed who participated in remembrance activities were grateful for the opportunities to speak about their babies and to heighten awareness of the tragedy that affects so many.

A Name for Baby

Names have meaning, and I'm not just talking about the meaning found in baby name books. Names provide identity, give substance and reality to a human life, and keep the memory of a person alive long after they leave this earth.[19] Even though I was halfway through the pregnancy with the first miscarriage, I was not able to learn my baby's gender after the delivery. It didn't occur to me at the time the positive impacts naming this baby may have had on my grieving process.

Forty-seven percent of the parents whom I interviewed named their babies, and for these parents, the act of naming their babies validated the lives of their children. A few mothers noted that there was an element of comfort in being able to call their children by their names whenever they spoke about them. One mother told me, "Naming the child was a part of the healing and [was] encouraged by those with similar loss." Another mother described the importance and consolation of hearing people mention her son's name in conversation:

> Some said things like, "[Baby's name] will always be in our hearts!" It meant so much to me to know that someone else would carry the memory of my son with me—that when the event faded and people forgot, I wouldn't be the only one remembering.

The parents I interviewed who named their babies believed they were worthy of names and recognition, and length of life had no bearing on the decision to give these babies names.[20] I recommend that you consider the implications of bestowing a name upon your baby as well. Even if there is no birth certificate on which to affix a name, you may find that naming your child is an important step in keeping Baby's memory alive.

My final note on the significance of naming babies is best related in the words of one of the mothers I interviewed who miscarried her first child at 24 weeks. Two years after losing her son (whose name is honored in necklaces worn by both Mama and Grandma), and after many months of stressful and difficult infertility treatments, this mother conceived again via invitro fertilization. When medical testing revealed the embryo was female, the parents gave their daughter a name before she was even implanted within the uterus. This mother explained the reasons behind naming the baby at this early stage:

> We felt that it made things feel "real" for us. It made her part of our family immediately, not waiting until she was born to give her a name. Pregnancy after loss is a rollercoaster of emotions, and even though we were joyful, it was also very stressful since we were acutely aware of the long list of things that could go wrong or lead to another loss. I also think that giving her a name helped me process the experience of pregnancy differently (compared to my pregnancy with [the first baby]).

What an astounding testimony! This couple named their daughter at a point when many people would not have even considered her a human being, but the parents' actions embody how our Heavenly Father viewed us at the same stage: "Your eyes saw my substance, being yet unformed, and in Your book they all were written, the days fashioned for me, when as yet there were none of them."[21] These parents did not simply see "a fertilized egg"—they saw a human being with life and potential, and they gave her a name.

Acknowledging your baby's loss as a death in the family is an important step in your healing process for a variety of reasons. It helps you to put the loss of your child into perspective, allows you the right to assert your parenthood, and gives you the freedom to grieve as you see fit. The life of your child is worthy of being acknowledged, and his or her passing is equally so. Honoring your baby with a memorial will encourage others to speak more openly about your loss and will help keep the memory of your child alive. Believe me, I understand the emotional and physical toll honoring Baby's memory may take, but claiming ownership of your parental grief decreases pain's hold upon your heart and helps foster healing.[22]

Unfortunately, however, outside influences may impede your ability to express grief. Maybe the opinions or words of medical professionals and/or family and friends created confusion about the reality of your Baby's humanness, or perhaps the words or behavior of certain individuals prevented you from freely articulating your loss. Whatever the reason, an inability to speak of Baby or outwardly mourn prolongs the grieving process in ways that are unhealthy physically, emotionally, and spiritually.

I learned this the hard way.

---

1. Kübler-Ross, *On Death and Dying*, 34.

2. If you are in this group, I encourage you to go to the Word of God, write down any scriptures that minister to you, and pray for the Lord to reveal to you His truth regarding the humanity of your child.

3. John 8:31–32.

4. Cacciatore et al., "When a Baby Dies," 452.

5. Cha and Thomas, "A Time of Healing," 1718.

6. Farren et al., "Posttraumatic Stress, Anxiety and Depression Following Miscarriage," 367.e9. Farren et al. found that psychological impacts were great among women who lost babies in early pregnancy or due to ectopic pregnancies: "One month after early pregnancy loss, we observed high proportions of women who met the criteria for posttraumatic stress (29%), moderate/severe anxiety (24%), and moderate/severe depression (11%). Although the prevalence of each disorder declined over time, observed proportions remained high 9 months after early pregnancy loss (18% for posttraumatic stress, 17% for moderate/ severe anxiety, 6% for moderate/severe depression)."

7. Boss, *Ambiguous Loss*, 3; Cacciatore et al., "When a Baby Dies," 443.

8. Several of the reasons for outsiders' failure to acknowledge infant loss are covered in Chapter 3.

9. Howlett, "Creating Meaningful Memorials."

10. Daniel, "Adding a New Dimension to Grief."

11. Mitima-Verloop et al., "Facilitating Grief," 735.

12. Jaffe and Diamond, "Grieving a Reproductive Loss"; Lang et al., "Perinatal Loss"; Mcgee et al., "Ambiguous Loss."

13. Lang et al., "Perinatal Loss," 189.

14. Mitima-Verloop et al., "Facilitating Grief," 736.

15. Jones, "Parental Identity in Narratives of Grief."; LeDuff III et al., "Transitional Objects to Facilitate Grieving."

16. Reagan, Proclamation No. 5890.

17. *Black's Medical Dictionary*, under "SIDS." Sudden Infant Death Syndrome, now known as Sudden Unexpected Death in Infancy.

18. Carlson, "Ways to Commemorate October 15," para. 2.

19. Because I like surprises, I was (apparently) one of the few women in the Western world who didn't take the opportunity to learn my babies' gender at my ultrasound appointments and had, therefore, not chosen names by the time of each loss.

20. The babies who received names ranged in age from 6 weeks to 27+ weeks' gestation.

21. Ps. 139:16.

22. Zhou et al., "The Relationship between Social Acknowledgment and Prolonged Grief Symptoms."

CHAPTER THREE

When Others Don't (or Won't) Acknowledge Baby's Loss

Reproach has broken my heart,
And I am full of heaviness;
I looked for someone to take pity,
but there was none;
And for comforters, but I found none.
PSALM 69:20

BABY THREE HAD BEEN a surprise (my daughter was just six months old when I became pregnant the third time, and we hadn't been trying to conceive), but after waiting for the recommended amount of time after that miscarriage, one of my primary goals had been to have another baby. It took nearly a year, so Eric and I were elated when I finally became pregnant with Baby Four. I made an early appointment to see my OB just to make sure everything was okay because one of the most painful parts of my first miscarriage was not knowing why it happened. The doctors could find no medical condition that explained the loss, so we had simply been told that it was "just one of those things." This time around, I wasn't taking any chances.

At eight weeks' gestation, my doctor performed an ultrasound in her office and quickly found the baby. "Everything looks good," she said with a big smile. She knew we had been trying to have another baby, and she had been very kind and comforting throughout the medical procedures that followed our first loss, so she was nearly as delighted as we were by this pregnancy.

Unfortunately, a few days later, I began to bleed. I called my doctor's office, and the nurse told me to go to the local imaging facility. Shortly after we arrived, I was again lying on a gurney next to an ultrasound machine.

The details about the ultrasound technician's appearance remain as unremarkable in my memory as his demeanor was to me that day. Everything about his behavior reflected a sense of routine. No smile. No small talk. Just the sounds of fingers tapping on a computer keyboard and the occasional clicking of the device capturing images on the screen.

"You already miscarried," he said at last with indifference and without preamble.

"That's impossible!" I replied, stunned. "I think I would have noticed. I just started bleeding a little while ago." There had been some bright-red blood, but my body had expelled nothing else that indicated a miscarriage.

"Well, there is nothing in your uterus, and there is nothing in your fallopian tube, so yes, you have miscarried," he said with clinical finality. This was an event that was evidently not terribly uncommon in his workaday life.

For me, however, this was anything but routine, and his recommendation that I go home to let my body "complete the process" left me heartbroken.

The remainder of that day is a fog in my mind, but I do remember that in the wee hours of the next morning, I was awakened by pain in my lower abdomen.

Eric's day had been as traumatic as mine, so I let him continue sleeping while I prayed silently, *Lord, this hurts so much! Please, please help me through this!*

As the hours passed, the cramping became more intense—delivering my first two children didn't hold a candle to this. Muffling my cries, I writhed on the damp sheets and rocked my legs back and forth in an effort to ease the pain.

Eric's a light sleeper, so it didn't take long for him to wake up and recognize something was wrong. He called the emergency exchange, and they notified my OB who called us quickly and sent me back for another ultrasound. We were at the facility as soon as the doors were open.

As the technician pressed the imaging wand over my uterus, I moaned and began to cry. The pain—both physical and emotional—was too intense. After just a few minutes, she quietly excused herself from the room.

This can't be good, I thought.

A tall, sandy-haired doctor entered. "Morning," he murmured, "I'm Dr. Jones."[1] Picking up the ultrasound wand, he dragged it over my lower torso to check my ovaries.

"You have a large mass in your abdomen," he said, focusing on the screen, "and it wasn't there at your last ultrasound. You need to go to the hospital."

Eric and I stared at Dr. Jones, wide-eyed, in silence. "What is it?" Eric finally asked huskily.

"I'm not quite sure." The doctor's words hung in the air as his eyes moved from Eric's alarmed expression to mine. Glancing back at the monitor, he quickly added, "It's not cancer; it's grown too quickly. It's about the size of a grapefruit now, and it wasn't there yesterday."

Eric muttered something about going home to pack a bag and arranging babysitting for our son and daughter when the doctor turned sharply toward him, saying sternly, "Do not go home. Don't go anywhere else. Go straight to the ER from here. I will call your OB and explain what is going on."

Things had suddenly taken a very serious turn for the worse.

My OB met us at the hospital and told us it looked like I'd had an ectopic pregnancy which required emergency surgery. She explained this would be a relatively short and not terribly invasive, laparoscopic procedure, during which she would insert a tiny camera through one small incision and remove the mass through another. As I lay on the operating table a short while later, my OB held my hand, and with dark, expressive eyes just visible over the top of the surgical mask that muffled her voice, she said soothingly, "I'm very sorry, Cheri."

I just wanted the pain to be over—I wanted all of this to be over, but I begged her to save my ovary if possible. Because I ovulated more from my left ovary than my right, I knew losing that ovary would decrease my chances of getting pregnant in the future. She said she would do her best, and the last thing I remembered before they put me under was the worried look in her eyes as the oxygen mask was placed over my nose and mouth.

When I finally awakened many hours later, I was lying on a bed in the surgical wing of the hospital, and Eric was asleep on a cot next to me. Caving to curiosity, I lifted the blanket and pulled up my hospital gown to see what the incisions looked like. Instead of the two small bandages I expected, medical tape held down a single swathe of thick gauze that extended from one side of my pelvis to the other.

"They couldn't do a laparoscopy," Eric suddenly said in a low, hoarse voice. The rustling of my blankets had evidently roused him from sleep. "They had to open you up."

I lowered the blankets and slowly turned my head to meet his gaze. He looked haggard, and his brow furrowed as the words came haltingly. "They had to take your ovary and fallopian tube."

My head dropped back onto the pillow, and tears immediately flowed. "What happened?"

"The doctor said the baby had attached to the ovary, not in the uterus. That's why they couldn't find anything in your uterus or fallopian tubes." He paused and then said, "I knew something was wrong when the surgery took three hours longer than expected."

I stared at his tear-filled eyes and read in them the worry and stress he'd been under. I reached out and squeezed his hand while we cried together.

My OB later told me that in her thirty-five years of practice, she had never seen this type of ectopic pregnancy (one where the egg implanted outside of the uterus but not within the fallopian tube), and she'd never had to perform a surgery quite like mine.

Lucky me. Another pregnancy loss with no explanation as to why it had happened. Heavy with grief and frustration, I felt let down by medical science yet again, but the scarcity of answers wasn't the only source of pain during that hospital stay.

Although my OB was as kind and comforting as she could be during her morning rounds, the other doctors and nurses who attended to me were any-thing but compassionate. Maybe it was because I wasn't recuperating on the labor and delivery floor, maybe it was the luck of the draw, or maybe it was that I lost the baby just under nine-weeks' gestation. Whatever the reason, the treatment I received with this early miscarriage was vastly different from when I lost my other baby at twenty weeks.

At no time after my surgery and subsequent hospital stay did any of my nurses give a single indication that they knew I had lost a baby. No one said they were sorry, no one mentioned the baby, and no one seemed to care that my pain was more than physical.

The morning after my procedure, a nurse stood at the foot of my bed. "You needed to get up and walk around," she said with a huff. If ever a voice had its hands on its hips, hers did.

Noting her conspicuous failure to offer to help me out of bed, I lay still. *I totally get that this is a part of recovery from surgery*, I thought as I glared at her through half-opened eyes, carrying on an internal dialogue that I was too weary and grief-stricken to speak aloud, *but I have zero desire to get out of bed, and you are just plain rude!*

The nurse turned and left the room, never returning to take me for the aforementioned walk.

The bulk of the interactions I had with hospital staff during this stay con-sisted of taking my vitals, adjusting my bed, and asking questions about the functioning of my bowels and quantity of flatulence. (I now know that these things indicated that my intestines were up and running again, but at the time, it just seemed insensitive given the reason for my surgery.)

After my first miscarriage, hospital staff provided compassionate care, but the nurses this time around showed little concern for anything but my physical condition. Hurt and confused by this lack of sympathy and refusal to mention Baby, I left the hospital with compounded sorrow.

Medical Perspectives of Pregnancy and Perinatal loss

Do not for a moment believe that the differences in the levels of compassion I received after my miscarriages were particular to me.

My research uncovered a common denominator in the way parents who experienced infant loss were treated by medical personnel: Typically, the earlier the pregnancy loss, the less sympathy parents received. For example, scientists from the Department of Thanatology[2] at Marian University in Wisconsin found that women who lost babies in the third trimester received more compassion from healthcare workers than mothers who miscarried in the first two trimesters, causing the latter group to feel "isolation, disenfranchised grief, and lack of recognition of their losses."[3] In another study of the miscarriage experiences of 596 women, scientists found that a staggering 49% felt stigmatized by healthcare workers who "did not recognize the significance of [their] loss" or who made "insensitive comments about how [they] should feel, grieve, or experience the loss."[4]

This difference in the ways medical staff treat perinatal loss indicates their sense that the grief evoked by miscarriages in the first half of pregnancy is not as genuine, intense, or worthy of recognition. For example, 21 of the 24 babies lost to the parents I interviewed were miscarried between 6–22 weeks' gestation, yet only 29% of these losses prompted condolences from hospital staff, and a mere 20% of these parents were provided with information on support groups or resources for dealing with infant loss.[5] However, 100% of the parents who experienced perinatal loss 24 weeks and beyond received sympathy from healthcare workers, and all these parents were provided with grief resources.

Several parents I interviewed who lost babies in the first or second trimesters also received little to no recognition of their grief and felt stigmatized by healthcare workers. A nurse told one woman I interviewed, "It's okay! You are young. You will have more children." This flippant comment after her miscarriage merely added to the mother's pain: "It made it seem as if the child was insignificant. Like the life didn't matter, and I was blowing it out of proportion." Another mother told me that she was left alone in her hospital room for hours on end, receiving little acknowledgment of her loss and no words of consolation during the two days it took to deliver her stillborn baby at sixteen weeks' gestation.

Dehumanizing Babies Lost to Miscarriage

One reason for such seeming indifference to parents' pain is likely healthcare workers' notion of the viability of a pregnancy. You see, if a "pregnancy is expected to continue developing normally," or if "a fetus might survive outside of the uterus" (with or without medical intervention), it is considered *viable.*[6] Problems arise when parents view miscarriage as the death of a baby while medical practitioners consider it simply to be an unviable pregnancy and then convey this belief (intentionally or unintentionally) to their patients. Parents may also become confused about how to feel, and/or they may get the impression "that their loss [is] insignificant to others" when healthcare workers use scientific jargon to refer to the pregnancy and fail to call the life within the womb a "baby."[7] (See Appendix C for detailed information on medical terminology and definitions for babies, miscarriage, and stillbirth.)

Many of the parents I interviewed described their experiences with doctors' use of medical terminology as hurtful, and it was clear to me that the passage of time had not dulled the sting of their words. One mother who miscarried at 9+ weeks told me that she was informed by an emergency department doctor that her "pregnancy was probably terminating" and that she should "go home and put [her] feet up and hope for the best." Another mother whose baby had implanted in a fallopian tube rather than in her uterus, explained how doctors continually referred to her baby only as an "ectopic pregnancy." Not once did they mention her loss or offer the mother sympathy, and her grief was extreme because she'd dealt with infertility for many years prior to this pregnancy. She told me, "I think I was just another surgery patient to them."

The negative effects of the use of scientific terms were also detailed in a recent Canadian study on miscarriage.[8] Several parents in this study described painful, insensitive encounters with healthcare providers, with one mother expressing her anger and frustration over her doctor's use of the word "abortion" to describe the death of her baby at 26 weeks' gestation:

> I got affected...when [the doctor] said, "You had an abortion." ...I kind of looked at her like: "What?" And she says, "It's just a term." And I got mad. That's the only time I got mad. I said, "Change your 'terms' cause it's not an abortion....It's not an abortion to me."[9]

Perhaps medical staff believe they are alleviating parents' pain by minimizing the humanness of babies lost to miscarriage, but for many parents, this often increases suffering.

The same idea applies when healthcare workers use scientific jargon to refer to the bodies and the disposal of miscarried babies. One perinatal study reported how painful it was to parents when their babies' "remains were ... treated more like biomedical waste than a baby who had died"; parents felt this treatment was "dehumanizing."[10]

A father I interviewed who lost six babies between 18- and 22-weeks' gestation described the heartbreaking manner in which the body of one of his infants was disposed.[11] The physician told this father and his wife that because the D and C performed on their 22-week-old baby had "damaged the fetus," the doctor would record its age as "under 20 weeks" so they wouldn't have to bury it.[12] (In the state in which this event occurred, babies 22 weeks and older required burial.) This father stated that he and his wife viewed this alteration in documentation "as being compassionate in the moment." Shortly afterward, however, the father felt disappointment at being denied the opportunity to provide a burial.

When I awoke from the D and C after my miscarriage at twenty weeks, one of the first questions I asked my doctor was, "Where is my baby?"

It wasn't difficult to interpret her distressed expression as she said hesitantly, "Well...the baby had passed away...and there was a lot of decomposition..."

She didn't complete her sentence, and I didn't ask anything more even though I secretly questioned her explanation because I had felt the baby move a few days before I had had the procedure. I believe this was my doctor's attempt to spare my feelings by shielding me from the truth of what took place during the D and C.

To this day, I regret that I was not given more advice about my medical options after the baby died because I could have made a more informed decision about what course of action to take. Frankly, I don't remember being given any options. It was like, "This is what needs to be done," and I went along because I trusted the professionals. I wish more of the medical staff had recognized that even though the heart of what they called a "fetus" was no longer beating, I may have instead chosen to deliver my baby, to learn the gender, to see him or her, and to say a proper goodbye. This wouldn't have been easy, but it may have removed many of the elements of the unknown and lessened a bit of my heartache over this miscarriage.

Like many of the parents I described, you may have also experienced confusion or frustration as a result of conversations with medical staff after your loss. Nothing can be done about what happened to you in the past, but going forward, request that others, including healthcare workers, refer to your loss and any future pregnancies as "babies." Advocate for yourself and your child. When you do so, you legitimize the life of your baby, your status as a parent, and the sorrow you feel.

Compassionate Care

Not all medical personnel are unsympathetic to parents' suffering, however, and when doctors and nurses acknowledge the lives of miscarried babies, parents are better comforted and feel that their right to grieve is validated. This acknowledgment may be as simple as healthcare workers' use of the word "baby" to help parents feel "more prepared for the realities of the birth experience, both physically and emotionally [which has] a positive impact on their longer-term experiences of grief."[13] Parents' mourning processes get a head start when there is greater understanding of what is actually happening and the free expression of grief is encouraged.

For a few of the parents I interviewed, medical personnel went over and above to express their condolences. One mother greatly appreciated the sympathy cards sent by hospital staff shortly after she left the hospital and again at Christmas (the time near her original due date). Two other mothers mentioned that they and their spouses were comforted by the kindness and compassion of healthcare workers while at the hospital, with one woman emphasizing the many ways staff facilitated her grieving process:

> The hospital made our baby available to us throughout our stay, and it felt like they went out of their way to accommodate us, with bringing our son back to us if requested, allowing more than the usual number of "visitors" in my labor and delivery room, and even more when I was in post-partum.

The efforts of these staffers went a long way in aiding the healing of their patients' minds as well as bodies. Memories of such compassionate care blessed these parents long after they left the hospital.

"Personhood" and Grief

I cannot lay all the blame for unsympathetic perspectives of perinatal loss at the feet of medical science; no, people's confusion about the grief associated with miscarriage is also influenced by cultural perspectives and laws. For example, "personhood" status,[14] or "the quality or condition of being an individual person" is denied to lives within the womb in 44 states within the US.[15] Personhood classifications are a big deal because they dictate whether birth, death, and stillbirth certificates are issued.

The significance of these documents should not be underestimated because for most grieving parents, a legal record of their baby's life and death provides a sense of legitimacy of their babies' existence.[16] One woman in a recent study explained how receiving a death certificate for her son impacted her: "I don't know what it is about having his name written somewhere that makes him any more real, but it does. Like, the first time I went in and saw his name, I was like, '[O]h! He was real! His name is somewhere!'"[17]

I did not receive a death certificate for either baby lost to miscarriage, including the one lost at 20 weeks. I sometimes wonder if a stillborn certificate would have been issued if I had delivered the baby rather than having a D and C. Legal certification would have meant a lot to me. It would have documented my baby's time on earth, revealed my baby's gender, and recorded my baby's name—a name that could have been added to our family tree.

Unfortunately, legal documentation of miscarriage was also a rare occurrence for the parents whom I interviewed. Of the 11 babies who were miscarried between 12–22 weeks' gestation, only one received a stillbirth and death certificate. One mother received a death certificate for her son who was born at 24 weeks and lived for 2 minutes. Another mother received a certificate of stillbirth for her son who was delivered at 27 weeks and 5 days. Although many of the parents I interviewed did not consider certificates necessary for their babies who were fewer than 20 weeks' gestation, one mother said she would have appreciated this record, indicating that it would have validated her baby's life to her and others.

Validation of your baby's life is what is needed to progress through the healing process, and if you did not receive legal recognition or acknowledgement from healthcare workers, family, or friends, do not allow this to add one more crack in an already fragile heart. Take this pain to the Lord and remember that the greatest validation of Baby's existence is found in the Word of God.

Although you are taking the first steps toward healing, know that there may still be days when you will cry out to the Lord with groanings too deep for words. When those days come, and as often as they come, remember that God has provided a way to not only bring you through your grief but to heal your broken heart. In Part 2 of this book, I explain your Heavenly Father's step-by-step process for expressing your true emotions and for receiving comfort from the Lord. This procedure—this precious gift provided by the Lord for mourning loss—is called *lamentation*.

---

1. The doctor's name has been changed for privacy.

2. American Psychological Association, "Thanatology," in *APA Dictionary of Psychology*, 1079. *Thanatology* is "the study of death and death-related behaviors, thoughts, feelings, and phenomena."

3. Domogalla et al., "Rural Perinatal Loss: A Needs Assessment," 1057.

4. Watson et al., "Pregnancy and Infant Loss," 6.

5. It should be noted that of the 20% of parents who received grief support, two were nurses who were consoled by their colleagues, and one of the parents (whose baby was lost at 20 weeks' gestation) held a funeral service and burial for her infant.

6. "Facts Are Important: Understanding and Navigating Viability," American College of Obstetricians and Gynecologists, updated 2026, para. 3–4, https://www.acog.o rg/advocacy/facts-are-important/understanding-and-navigating-viability.

7. Lang et al., "Perinatal Loss," 191; Cassidy, "The Disenfranchisement."

8. Lang et al., "Perinatal Loss."

9. Lang et al., "Perinatal Loss," 191.

10. Lang et al., "Perinatal Loss," 189.

11. This was the only father to complete the questionnaire for this book. His wife at the time of these losses was not interviewed.

12. *Black's Medical Dictionary*, "Dilatation and Curettage," 187: "(Commonly referred to as D and C), a gynaecological operation to scrape away the lining of the uterus (endometrium). The procedure may be used to diagnose and treat heavy bleeding from the womb (endometriosis) as well as other uterine disorders. It can be used to terminate a pregnancy or to clean out the uterus after a partial miscarriage."

13. Smith et al., "Parents' Experiences of Care Following the Loss of a Baby," 871.

14. *Oxford English Dictionary*, "Personhood," 2015, https://www.oxfordreference.c om/search/search? source=%2F10.1093%2Facref%2F9780199571123.001.0001% 2Facref-9780199571123&q=personhood.

15. Idaho Statutes Title 32, Domestic Relations § 32-102, Unborn child as existing person (2025). As of this writing, US federal law designates the legal status of "personhood" to babies who show signs of life outside the womb (whether this life be minutes or years), but babies who die prior to 24 weeks within or outside the womb are not legally considered "persons." The good news is that by 2022, the states of California, Idaho, Louisiana, Montana, North Dakota, and South Dakota had conferred legal status upon fetuses within the womb, each state using language similar to that of my home state of Idaho: "A child conceived, but not yet born, is to be deemed an existing person, so far as may be necessary for its interests in the event of its subsequent birth."

16. Cacciatore et al., "From 'Silent Birth' to Voices Heard."; Fleming and Roth, *When Fetuses Gain Personhood*; Middlemiss, *Invisible Labours*.

17. Middlemiss, *Invisible Labours*, 90.

Part 2:

Lamenting Baby's Loss

MERRY HEART MINISTRIES

CHAPTER FOUR

Cry out to the Lord

Save me, O God! . . .
I am weary with my crying;
My throat is dry;
My eyes fail while I wait for my God.
PSALM 69:1, 3

"WHY, GOD? WHY? *WHY?!*"

The hot water ran over my head and face as I stood in the shower, pouring out my heart to the Lord, each word expressed with greater intensity until the last was a scream.

My husband was at work, and my young son and daughter were still asleep, so this was a chance to allow the emotions that had been fermenting just below the surface to spill out in what eventually became an eruption of grief. There weren't many opportunities to do so in the days following my first miscarriage. I had a three-year-old and one-year-old who needed my attention, a house to take care of, and a husband who was still grieving as well, both for his lost child and his wife who was clearly taking a very long time to get over this loss.

Not wanting to add to Eric's distress, I usually saved my outbursts for when he wasn't home. Don't get me wrong; my husband was—and still is—a rock for me, letting me soak his shirt with my tears as often as I needed, but as the months dragged on and on, the darkness of my mood did not seem to be lightening.

After we lost our first baby, discouragement and a mood of depression were my daily companions. The questions whirling around in my head were like a tornado: They started out small, but as they churned, they gathered momentum, pummeling what I thought were the giant redwoods of my faith, uprooting some, and tattering others. I often cried out to the Lord with questions that were far from respectfully articulated: "Where are You? Why did this happen? How could You allow this to happen? Don't You care? Haven't I served You faithfully? Have I done something wrong? Have I displeased You in some way?"

Initially, I was afraid to say these things aloud. It felt like a lack of faith in God to entertain these thoughts, much less to give them utterance. However, as the pain grew and the questions roiled inside, it seemed somehow dishonest to fail to admit them to the Lord. (I know that God already knows what's going on inside our hearts and minds, but I'm sure you catch my drift.) A few weeks after this miscarriage, I finally spoke up, and when I did, the questions gushed out as quickly as the water spewing out of the showerhead.

When we experience the loss of a loved one, including a tiny life within the womb, the intense pain of the situation often prompts us to cry out to the Lord in our distress. This is good. This is fitting. This is expected. After all, we are human, and our frustrations require an outlet. We have a deep-seated need for answers to our questions as well, often wanting to know the "why" of it all. Many Christians also want to know why bad things happen to those who are faithfully serving the Lord, and I had these same questions in the months and years following the loss of our babies.

Looking back, I now realize that my expectations of God's behavior (framed by my religious upbringing) are what led to my questioning the Lord after my miscarriages. You see, prior to my junior year of high school, my family had attended a church in a denomination that taught that God loved us and sent His Son to die for us, but I was also told things like, "Yes, Jesus's disciples performed wonderful miracles through the Holy Spirit in the first century, but that is not how the Lord does things these days." Therefore, when something awful (e.g., sickness, accident, death) befell someone we knew, I heard platitudes such as, "Well, it must have been God's will"—a notion that never made sense to me, especially since I'd been taught in Sunday School that the Lord was kind and merciful. These conflicting perceptions of God painted a rather confusing picture of my Father in heaven.

In my mid-teens, however, my aunt encouraged my family to visit the church she was attending. There, I learned that I was valuable and precious in God's sight and that the Lord is the same yesterday, today, and forever—what He did in the early days of the Church, He could and would do today.[1] I was also taught about the "benefits" of forgiveness, wholeness, and kindness that the Lord provides to His children:

> Bless the LORD, O my soul,
> And forget not all His *benefits*:
> Who forgives all your iniquities,
> Who heals all your diseases,
> Who redeems your life from destruction,
> Who crowns you with lovingkindness and tender mercies,
> Who satisfies your mouth with good things,
> So that your youth is renewed like the eagle's (emphasis added).[2]

These words boggled my mind! The God of heaven and earth cared enough about me not only to forgive my sins (this I had known for as long as I could remember), but He also wanted to bless me with good health, tender mercies, and renewed strength.

The problem was that in my spiritual and physical immaturity, I thought that if I stood on God's promises of blessing, troubles would either not come my way, or the Lord would set up a barrier to prevent them from hurting me: "For You, O Lord, will bless the righteous; With favor You will surround him as with a shield."[3] In my mind, troubles would always be repelled by the defenses the

Lord would surely set up around my life, much like Captain Kirk's deflector shields on the Starship Enterprise.

This naïve, perspective that the promises of God meant absence of tribulation had become an important element in the bedrock of my faith. Without realizing it, my faith had become what Christian author Kristen LaValley calls a "transactional" belief system.[4] Basically, I believed that because I had been faithful to God in serving Him, He would show His faithfulness to me with blessings and generally smooth sailing.

With this mindset, it is hardly surprising that when the storms of life hit in adulthood (financial difficulties as well as the loss of our two babies), I became confused and questioned God because He was not behaving according to the transactional formula of my expectations. My faith had become, as LaValley so aptly states it, self-centered rather than God-centered:

> When our image of God is dependent on things going the way we believe they should, our image of him is centered on us, not on him. But true faith isn't believing God is good just because we have proof of it. Faith is believing that he's good even when we don't have proof.[5]

You see, my incomplete knowledge of Scripture had, after my miscarriages, tainted my perception of God's character. I had forgotten that God is *always* good. Troubles are not evidence to the contrary.

I had also forgotten Jesus's warning that we still live in a fallen world where bad things happen to everyone, even followers of Christ: "These things I have spoken to you, that in Me you may have peace. In the world you will have tribulation; but be of good cheer, I have overcome the world."[6] Up through my late twenties, I had focused on the Lord's ultimate victory and the promise of peace contained in this scripture rather than His revelation that there will be trials in this life.[7]

Therefore, when incredible suffering came my way as an adult, I was ill-prepared for how to "be of good cheer" during difficult times. I wasn't even sure what that meant. The heartbreak of miscarriage did not seem like "all things work[ing] together for good for those who love the Lord," so I was devastated and felt like I had somehow lost the favor of the Lord.[8] Thus, for years after my miscarriages, I periodically cried out to the Lord while standing in my shower or face down in my closet, laying my confusion and feelings of rejection and abandonment at His feet.

Biblical Lamentation

God is so good and so faithful. Despite my mistaken perceptions of Him and my floundering in the "Cry out to the Lord" stage of mourning for many years longer than necessary, my Heavenly Father gently guided me toward the path of genuine recovery: biblical lamentation. My prayer for you, dear sister, is that the following explanation will also enable you to reap the benefits of the Lord's plan for grieving.

If you are unfamiliar with lamentation, allow me to explain its purpose as laid out in the Word of God. A modern definition of *lamentation* is "a passionate expression of grief" or to "mourn a person's death."[9] However, for followers of Christ, lamentation is more than crying or mourning a loss. Lamentation is a means of working through our grief before the Lord by using the language provided to us in His Word. In fact, it's been said that lamentation "should be the chief way Christians process grief in God's presence."[10]

The language of lamentation enables God's people to express their pain to the Lord while still standing on His Word—while still believing that God' Word is true during difficult circumstances and regardless of what their eyes see.[11] Lamentation is not simply a prayer expressed in times of trouble; it is a gift from the Lord to His children—His very human, very emotionally wrought children—to help them work their way through suffering and sorrow. It is an opportunity to turn to the Lord, tell Him about our problems, ask Him questions, and request help. Once we have done these things, it becomes easier to trust, wait upon, and praise Him.

The Purpose of Lamentation

Death—including infant loss—does not compartmentalize. Death does not select a tiny parcel of land within your life, neatly settle there, and keep to itself. Death is an obtrusive resident that encroaches on all the neighboring acreage, impacting the planting as well as the harvest of productive things. Therefore, do not expect that the loss of your child will not affect every area of your life, be it physical, emotional, relational, or spiritual. You had plans, dreams, and expectations for this little person, and your life will never be the same after Baby's passing.

This is why lamentation is so important. Christians should not "sorrow as others who have no hope" for two reasons: 1) We know that our loved ones are with the Lord and that we will one day be reunited, and 2) The Lord has provided within His Word a pattern for mourning.[12] Engaging in this process of lamentation will enable you to respond—rather than react—to your baby's loss by allowing the Holy Spirit to till the fallow soil of your heart, replenish essential nutrients, and plant the seeds of the Word of God. Lamentation encourages believers to submit themselves to the Master cultivator, and as a result of His oversight, the fruit of the Spirit will grow and flourish.

Regrettably, twenty-first century American Christians do not often possess the ability to mourn well (publicly or privately) because they haven't been taught about lamentation. Instruction about grief is rare in contemporary American churches, and in-depth teaching from the books of Psalms or Lamentations is even more infrequent.[13] In the latter, the prophet Jeremiah is mourning the destruction of Jerusalem, and there are a lot of expressions of pain and suffering, so this book of the Bible isn't one on which pastors are very eager to teach. Many Christians are also unlikely to read Lamentations on their own and/or read it all the way through because, to put it bluntly, if you're in a positive frame of mind, Lamentations is a downer. If you're in a period of grief, you may not be in the mood to read poems of sadness which you believe will increase rather than relieve your pain.

However, it is important to remember that the book of Lamentations and psalms of lamentation were placed in the Bible for a reason: Lamentation is vital in the development of our understanding of how to deal with grief. During times of suffering and struggle, Christians may doubt or forget the promises of God, "and lament provides the opportunity to re-orient your hurting heart toward what is true."[14] When we engage in lamentation, we get a clearer picture of God's omnipotence, strength, and wisdom, and this clarity makes us keenly aware our own frailty and lack of understanding while simultaneously boosting our trust in a faithful God.[15]

This "re-orienting" of our hearts toward truth should be the goal of lamentation in general and for lamenting the loss of our babies specifically, but the Lord knows it is difficult for us to accomplish this without getting rid of a lot of the crud that misdirects our attention and obstructs our progress. Therefore, our Heavenly Father provided us with templates for lamentation throughout His Word—some of the strongest templates of which are within the book of Psalms—to guide our healing processes during times of bereavement.

Through my research on grief, I discovered two particularly useful strategies for applying the principles of lamentation. The first strategy comes from pastor and author Mark Vroegop's book *Dark Clouds, Deep Mercy: Discovering the Grace of Lament,* and the second comes from author Jennifer Rothschild's Bible study on lament, "How Long, O Lord?" Each of these authors explains how they processed their grief after infant loss by following the structure of lamentation as described in the books of Lamentations and Psalms.[16] When I studied these texts for myself, the pattern of lament was so obvious, I could have kicked myself for failing to study these scriptures years ago! My desire is that you will benefit from the following synthesis of my study on lamentation. I pray that you will discover how our Heavenly Father provides for all our needs, including (dare I say, *especially*) the needs we have in times of suffering.

Pattern for Lamentation

I happen to like mnemonic devices because they help me to remember things. When I was a child, for example, mnemonic devices helped me to remember the answers to many a difficult test question as well as notes on the musical staff (e.g., E, G, B, D, F: Every Good Boy Does Fine). I have even used such devices as an adult to help me remember grocery lists and to teach rules of grammar.[17] Since this memory tool is so useful, I decided to conflate Vroegop and Rothschild's explanations of the lamentation structure to create a mnemonic device of my own to aid your ability to remember the steps of lamentation: Courageous Christians Really Rattle the Enemy (CCRRE).

- **C**ry out to the Lord.

- **C**omplain to and question the Lord.

- **R**equest of the Lord.

- **R**emember the Lord.

- **E**xpress trust and praise the Lord.

Now let's break down each element in the lamentation structure to demonstrate how this pattern of prayer may lead to a breakthrough in your grieving process.

Crying out to the Lord

When the storms of life come crashing down upon you, when you are battle-worn and feel unable to stand, when you are bruised, broken, and unsure where to turn, look to God for support. I do not say this flippantly; I say this because I know the world does not stop simply because you are experiencing tragedy. There are many things vying for your attention. You still have to go to work, feed the family, wash the clothes, and pay the bills. In the days following your loss, it may seem there is little opportunity to grieve. Even if—especially if—you are angry with God, you must make a conscious effort to shift your focus from your problems to the Lord. Cry out to Him for strength and deliverance, and "push the heart toward God in [y]our pain."[18]

In the midst of your heartache, comfort and support may feel far away, but trust me, your Heavenly Father desires to provide solace if you will only turn to Him. Remember, the apostle Paul described our Heavenly Father as "the Father of mercies and God of all *comfort*" (emphasis added).[19] Know that you are most definitely not alone in your feelings of abandonment. You are walking on a path well worn. For proof of this, look at how the various psalms of lamentation begin (see Appendix D for a few illustrations). Notice how each of these songs starts with the psalmists' turning to the Lord and letting their sorrows flow.

In song after song, the psalmists cry out in pain, disappointment, and desperation—reaching out, sometimes physically, to the Lord for help. Imagine the psalmist Asaph's hands reaching heavenward, tears streaming down his face in the wee hours as he makes his appeal to God: "In the day of my trouble I sought the Lord; My hand was stretched out in the night without ceasing; My soul refused to be comforted."[20]

Have you, like Asaph, felt there was no comfort for your soul? In the wake of your child's passing, how many times have you, like King David and the prophet Isaiah, cried out to the Lord, "How long, O Lord?"[21] How many sleepless nights have you spent begging God to step up the pace of the relief or pleaded with Him to listen to you, help you, or save you from your suffering?

The psalms of lamentation reveal that when we are weary with sorrow, turning to the Lord is the most effective way to deal with our feelings. Yes, we should also seek consolation from our spouses, family, and sisters and brothers in Christ, but God alone is the One who has all the answers, and God alone is capable of effectively addressing our pain. He yearns for His children to come to Him for help, and He has made this abundantly clear in His Word:

- "Therefore, the Lord longs to be gracious to you, And therefore He waits on high to have compassion on you. For the Lord is a God of justice; How blessed are all those who long for Him."[22]

- "Be anxious for nothing, but in everything by prayer and supplication, with thanksgiving, let your requests be made known to God; and the peace of God, which surpasses all understanding, will guard your hearts and minds through Christ Jesus."[23]

- "Therefore, humble yourselves under the mighty hand of God, that He may exalt you in due time, casting all your care upon Him, for He cares for you."[24]

- "Come to Me, all you who labor and are heavy laden, and I will give you rest."[25]

Dear sister, your Heavenly Father is waiting for you to come to Him with your pain. Turn to the Lord, get down on your knees or lie down on your face, and call out to your Heavenly Father in your distress. Then get ready to make your complaint.

---

1. Heb. 13:8.

2. Ps. 103:2–5.

3. Ps. 5:12.

4. LaValley, *Even if He Doesn't*, 33.

5. LaValley, *Even if He Doesn't*, 34.

6. John 16:33.

7. I believed at that time that the tribulation to which Jesus referred was for first-century disciples (many of whom were stoned, beaten, and martyred). By the way, I now fully recognize the irony of thinking that *tribulations* for Christians did not extend beyond the first century, but *blessings* for Christians did.

8. Rom. 8:28.

9. *Oxford English Dictionary*, under "lamentation."

10. Higginbottom, "Biblical Lament," para. 3.

11. Vroegop, *Dark Clouds, Deep Mercy*.

12. 1 Thess. 4:13.

13. There has been more emphasis on "feel-good" messages in churches and less teaching on the purpose and process of lamentation, and this needs to change if the Church is going to effectively deal with grief within the Body of Christ.

14. Vroegop, *Dark Clouds, Deep Mercy*, 38.

15. Higginbottom, "Biblical Lament."

16. Vroegop, *Dark Clouds, Deep Mercy*, 29. Vroegop's application of the following pattern enabled him to process the death of his daughter, lost a few days prior to her due date: A Turn to God, A Cry out to God, A Complaint, A Request, An Expression of Trust and/or Praise. Rothschild, "How Long, O Lord?," 119. Similarly, in her Bible study on prayers of lament, Rothschild explains how she created the mnemonic device, "APREP," as a memory aid for lamenting her miscarriage: Address God (Focus your prayer on the One who hears and answers); Pour out your heart (Bring Him your complaints and concerns); Request help (Ask God for what you need); Express Trust (Affirm your faith in His character and His Word); Praise Him (Worship Him because He is worthy).

17. FANBOYS is the mnemonic devise for the following coordinating conjunctions: for, and, nor, but, or, yet, so.

18. Vroegop, *Dark Clouds, Deep Mercy*, 30.

19. 2 Cor. 1:3.

20. Ps. 77:2.

21. Ps. 13:1; Isa. 6:11.

22. Isa. 30:18, NAS.

23. Phil. 4:6–7.

24. 1 Pet. 5:6–7.

25. Matt. 11:28. Strong, *Strong's Exhaustive Concordance*, under "G2872, *kŏpiaō*"; "G5412, *phŏrtizō*"; "G373, *anapauō*"; Yeivin and Rabinowitz, "Yoke," 381. The words "labor" and "heavy laden" are translated from the Greek words *kŏpiaō* and *phŏrtizō* which respectively mean "to toil, be wearied" and "to load or burden." The word translated as "rest" is from *anapauō* which means "to repose; to refresh." Bible scholars have long interpreted Jesus's words to mean that His followers should not labor under and be weighed down by other religious teachings, but Christians should instead turn to Him and take upon themselves His yoke of instruction. If disciples of Jesus do so, He promises, "[Y]ou will find rest for your soul. For My yoke is easy and My burden is light" (Matt. 11:29–30). In Jewish culture, "yoke" is a "symbol of service and servitude" to God and the teachings of the Torah, so this traditional interpretation makes sense. However, Jesus's words are typically multilayered in meaning, and this verse also likely indicates that when we are fatigued and are burdened with the cares of life—including grief from loss—our load will be lightened, and we will find rest when we turn to the teachings of Jesus. Thus, when we seek understanding from the Word of God, we will find the truth, and the truth will refresh our souls.

CHAPTER FIVE

Complain to and Question the Lord

For my soul is full of troubles,
And my life draws near to the grave.
PSALM 88:3

I FELT HOLLOW. EMPTY. Strangely alone. A few days before my first miscarriage, there had been two hearts beating within me, and the thudding of my own heart beating in my ears reminded me there was now only one—just one—and this void within me was not filled with a bundle of joy in my arms. I cried often, crying until I had no more tears, and then I groaned, wordlessly rocking back and forth with my arms wrapped around my waist as I sat on my bed or on the couch, waiting for the pain to subside. In the early days of loss, I often had no voice. There were simply no words.

Once the reality of the situation sank in, however, it was difficult to stem the tide of words, questions, and expressions of sorrow. I began to cry out to the

Lord, and these cries quickly turned to complaint: "Where were You, God? Why didn't You prevent this from happening? My baby...died!"

Pain prompts questions and evokes confusion and anger, and sometimes, even for Christians, our negative feelings are directed toward God. If you have found yourself crying out in grief like this, take heart! Your feelings are not unusual, and you are not alone in needing to vent your emotions and ask questions. The book of Psalms is filled with the cries of people suffering under tremendous strain, and after these psalmists turn to the Lord in their pain, they lay out their complaints, explaining in detail what is happening to them. To give you a sense of what I am talking about, see table 1 for a few examples of the ways that David complained to the Lord.

TABLE 1. David's Problems and Complaints

David's Problem	David's Complaint
His enemies are surrounding him.	"Many are they who rise up against me" (Ps. 3:1).
His enemies are trying to kill him.	"They gather together, they hide, they mark my steps, when they lie in wait for my life" (Ps. 56:6).
People are ridiculing him.	"But I am a worm, and no man; a reproach of men, and despised by the people" (Ps. 22:6).
	"I became a byword to them....And I am the song of the drunkards" (Ps. 69:11–12).
He is afraid and wishes he could disappear to escape his pain.	"Fearfulness and trembling have come upon me, and horror has overwhelmed me. Oh, that I had wings like a dove! I would fly away and be at rest" (Ps. 55:5–6).
He is physically and emotionally exhausted from trying to escape his enemies.	"I am weary with my groaning; All night I make my bed swim; I drench my couch with my tears. My eye wastes away with grief" (Ps. 6:6–7).

Although David was not sinless, he was considered "a man after God's own heart," so we should pay attention to the way in which David laments.[1] If you examine the psalms of lamentation, you will see that in most of them, David spends a great deal of time complaining to the Lord by explaining to Him what is happening in his life. In my estimation, if our Heavenly Father was okay with David's complaints, He will be okay with yours and mine.

Complaint Versus Grumbling

Although the Lord welcomes our complaints, we should also be mindful of David's *approach* when complaining and model our own prayers of lamentation after his. Psalm 77 provides an excellent illustration of the correct way to complain: "I remembered God, and was troubled; I complained, and my spirit was overwhelmed.... I call to remembrance my song in the night: I commune with mine own heart: and my spirit made diligent search."[2] The words "complained" and "commune" are both translated from the same Hebrew word, *sîyach,* which means "to ponder, converse with or utter; to talk, meditate, speak, pray, commune, or declare."[3] Thus, David's style of complaining is a lot like how people would share with a spouse, beloved family member, or friend their innermost feelings regarding life's troubles.

David's lament also indicates honesty and intimacy: He searches his heart, analyzes his situation, and then shares with the Lord how he feels. The important point you need to remember is that although David complained about his circumstances, he did not *grumble*: He did not brood over his problems or accuse God of not knowing what He was doing, and neither did David shake his fist at God—literally or figuratively.

Now contrast David's communion with the Lord with the method of complaint used by the Israelites in the desert about a year and a half after they left Egypt.[4] (This may feel like a bit of a detour, but I promise it is important.) In Numbers 14:27, the Lord said to Moses and Aaron, "How long shall I bear with this evil congregation who complain [*lûwn*] against Me? I have heard the complaints [*telûnah*] which the Children of Israel make against Me."[5] The

Israelites stubbornly continued in a routine of obstinate grumbling (or as I call it, "griping"), and the kicker is that this was done privately to one another and possibly (probably) under their breath. Evidence for their inward grumbling is found in Psalm 78:17–18: "But they sinned even more against Him by rebelling against the Most High in the wilderness. *And they tested God in their heart* by asking for the food of their fancy" (emphasis added).

The Lord God Almighty who sees the condition of the hearts and minds of each of His children was angry with the Israelites because they didn't believe He would take care of them.[6] Instead of trusting in the Lord and remembering the numerous and wonderful ways He had shown them His love throughout the previous year (being spared from ten plagues, crossing the Red Sea on dry ground, and receiving water and manna in the desert come to mind), the Israelites doggedly stuck to their complaints that Moses had dragged them into the desert to die and that God didn't even care about them.

This behavior doesn't make sense until you consider the negative effects of the Israelites' griping. As Rothschild explains, grumbling "speaks against rather than leaning toward [God]. It pulls back rather than presses in."[7] It is unclear if the children of Israel actually believed their complaints were accurate, if murmuring about difficulties became a habit they chose not to break, or if grumbling gave them a sense of superiority over Moses, but whatever the case, their complaining was a form of speaking against God that ultimately separated them from Him. This occurred verbally at first, but the separation became physical as well when they were not allowed into the Promised Land.[8]

The Israelites' fate is a warning to Christians today about the detriments of grumbling about the character of God and failing to trust in Him. If we want God's presence in our lives and His help in our circumstances, we must bolster our trust in the Lord by remembering what He has already done for us.

Dear sister, keep these thoughts in mind as you approach the Lord to complain about your circumstances. Use David as your model. Lay your complaints before the Lord with an attitude of humility—the same attitude you would expect a child to show toward an adult. Make your complaint known to Him, but be sure to maintain respect for the Lord.

"Be Angry and Do Not Sin"

For many more months than I care to admit, I was angry with the Lord for not preventing the deaths of my children, and I know some of you may have felt the same way. Human beings are rather good at being angry with God when things don't go as we expect or want them to. We know God has the power to save and restore life, so when He doesn't, indignation often rears its ugly head.

Case in point: My father-in-law, Roger, has candidly shared how frustration with the Lord manifested itself when his sixteen-year-old son, Craig, died following a horrific car accident. As Craig lingered on life support for several days, my parents-in-law and their church family prayed for Craig, believing wholeheartedly that God would heal and restore his life. The day Craig passed away, numerous friends filled the Halvorson home to console the family, but when Roger was left alone, anger erupted in a cry of frustration with the Lord.

Hurling his Bible across the living room, Roger bellowed, "Your promises aren't worth a crap! I'll trust you for salvation because I don't want to go to hell, but I won't trust you for anything else!"

Fortunately, Roger didn't stay in this mode of anger for long. He humbled himself before his Heavenly Father, apologized for his outburst, and went on to develop an even stronger relationship with the Lord, eventually going into the ministry. Much like what happened with my father-in-law, disappointment of our expectations combined with the heartbreak of death has the potential to spark outrage within the most fervent servant of the Lord. The key is to remember the biblical principles for dealing with anger.

You see, the Bible doesn't tell us that anger itself is wrong, but God's Word does explain that what we do with that anger could have negative consequences, especially when the anger is directed at God. When the apostle Paul explains Psalm 4:4 to the Christians in Ephesus, he clarifies the problem with hanging onto anger: "'Be angry but do not sin': do not let the sun go down on your wrath, nor give place to the devil."[9] Letting anger brew and stew opens the door to our enemy and sin. It is a submission to the devil rather than a submission to

God that, much like an injured animal in pain that bites the hand of the one tending the wounds, causes us to lash out at God instead of our enemy—the one who is truly responsible for our pain.

Pent up anger may also cause us to ignore the Lord entirely which is a form of desperation that has dire spiritual ramifications:

> Giving God the silent treatment is the ultimate manifestation of unbelief. Despair lives under the hopeless resignation that God doesn't care, he doesn't hear, and nothing is ever going to change. People who believe this stop praying. They give up.[10]

Even in your grief over your little one, don't give up on God, dear sister! Do not give Him the cold shoulder or allow the enemy to rob you of your intimacy with the Lord, for He sees you in your desert of grief, and He knows exactly how to provide for your every need.

Maintaining Reverence in Your Complaint

Throughout the lamentation process, we must also maintain our sense of awe of the God of the heavens and the earth. If you are reading this now and thinking of a time when you may not have been as respectful to the Lord as you should have been, let me encourage you. We have a very merciful God who is quick to forgive when we come to Him with a penitent heart.[11] If you need a reminder of the ever-lasting mercy of our Lord, check out Psalm 136; all 26 verses of this psalm end with the phrase, "For His mercy endures forever." If this is not encouragement enough, let us look at a couple of men in Scripture who had to be reminded of God's sovereignty when, during lamentation, they were disrespectful of the Lord.

Job's Complaints and Revelation

We will start out by looking at the story of Job. In all frankness, if anyone had reason to complain, it was Job. All his children and livestock were killed, and both his wealth and health were lost despite being head of the class in righteousness and respect for the Lord. God Himself says of Job, "[T]here is none like him on the earth, a blameless and upright man, one who fears God and shuns evil."[12] For these reasons, it did not make much sense to Job that he was enduring such tribulation, and for these same reasons, people still wonder at the severity of God's tone when He finally speaks to Job toward the end of the book. However, if we look at the style of Job's lament, we will find some clues as to the content of and the reasons for the Lord's response to him.

Prior to God's answer to Job, there is a lengthy back and forth between Job and his friends which has prompted multiple books and sermons, but for the purposes of this chapter, I will give you the problems with Job's lament in a nutshell. Rather than turning to God in his distress, Job begins by cursing the day he was born.[13] Rather than crying out to the Lord, Job says he is not smart enough to talk to God, and even if he were given a chance to speak, "surely he would be swallowed up."[14] Rather than laying out his complaint to the Lord, Job explains his miseries in detail to his friends and begs them to pity him. Rather than making his requests known to God, Job answers his friends' questions and accusations—most of which were wrong in so many ways—with justifications of his own righteousness and knowledge of the Lord. He even goes so far as to blame God for his woes:

> If I called and He answered me,
> I would not believe that He was listening to my voice.
> For he crushes me with a tempest,
> And multiplies my wounds without cause.[15]

These two verses are buried in the middle of chapter nine, but they are a telling indication of Job's real problems. Grief and distress have consumed Job to the extent that he has failed to turn to the Lord, and this failure to seek God's face in the middle of the greatest storm of his life has skewed Job's perception of God's character because He doesn't believe God would answer him if he were to call to Him, and He views God as sadistic and uncaring.

Thus, the Lord's response. Since Job has forgotten who his God is, the Lord reminds him in no uncertain terms that He is the Great I Am, He is the Creator, He is in charge, and He is the source of wisdom:

> Where were you when I laid the foundations of the earth?
> Tell Me, if you have understanding.
> Who determined its measurements?
> Surely you know!
> Or who stretched the line upon it?
> To what were its foundations fastened?
> Or who laid its cornerstone,
> When the morning stars sang together,
> And all the sons of God shouted for joy?[16]

The Lord expounds upon His omnipotence for four full chapters—not to make Job feel stupid or insignificant, but to give him greater understanding of the power and knowledge of the One to whom he should have run for comfort.

I really have to give Job kudos for his quick turn-around. His reply to the Lord indicates his humility, repentance, and acknowledgment of God's sovereignty:

> Therefore I have uttered what I did not understand,
> Things too wonderful for me, which I did not know....
> I have heard of You by the hearing of the ear,
> But now my eye sees You.[17]

Job now recognizes the inadequacy of his own wisdom in contrast with God's power and authority, so he admits he was speaking out of a lack of understanding when he tried to justify himself and accused God of being the source of his pain. The kicker is, once Job recognizes this, he is able to truly *see* God.

Asaph's Complaints and Revelation

Although Asaph may not be as well known as Job, his acknowledgment of and response to his faulty complaining is also worth noting. Coming from the tribe of Levi, Asaph was appointed by King David to minister before the ark of the covenant with songs of thanksgiving and praise, and he also authored twelve of the psalms, including Psalm 73.[18]

I like Psalm 73 because it is a good lesson in how to approach lament. I also like Asaph's honesty in this psalm, and I really like that he admits his envy, jealousy, and confusion of "the prosperity of the wicked."[19] However, what I most appreciate is Asaph's acknowledgment of the limits of his understanding and how this drives his humility and repentance for questioning God:

> Thus my heart was grieved,
> And I was vexed in my mind.
> I was so foolish and ignorant;
> I was like a beast before You.
> Nevertheless, I am continually with You;
> You hold me by my right hand.
> You will guide me with Your counsel,
> And afterward receive me to glory."[20]

Asaph recognizes that in comparison to the wisdom and knowledge of God, he is as clueless as a beast, and once he acknowledges this, the Lord is able to take him by the hand as a parent would a child, direct his path with good advice, and receive Asaph into His presence to provide the comfort he craves.

The Word of God reveals that our Heavenly Father knows His children are human and have a need to vent, but He desires that we bring our complaints to *Him*. However, when we do so, we should come with humility, remembering His authority, sovereignty, and ability to see and understand things far better than we are able.

It encourages me to find people in Scripture who feel as I do. Their fallibility makes them relatable, and although their stories are sometimes cautionary tales intended to help us avoid similar pitfalls, it is their very humanness that makes their good decisions seem achievable for the rest of us. I trust that the above examples of the Israelites, Job, and Asaph give you a sense of not just how to complain to your Heavenly Father but how to complain with reverence and respect for Him as well. Complaining in this manner will both aid your grieving process and draw you closer to the Lord.

Questioning the Purpose of the Storm

After my losses, I asked the Lord, "Why?" more times than I can count. As I mentioned at the beginning of this chapter, I had a lot of questions, but mainly, I wanted to know why my babies died. Were their deaths preventable? Was it something I ate or did?

The question, "Why?" haunted my dreams and my waking hours, but my pleas were met with (what I perceived to be) stoney silence. Zip. Nil. Nothing from the Lord on this, and in my ignorance and sense of entitlement, I got angry with Him. I related to the psalmist's anguished cries: "Do not hide your face from me when I am in distress. Turn your ear to me; when I call, answer me quickly."[21] I knew the Lord saw me and saw my anguish, so I could not understand why He was not answering me.

I believed that if I could just find the answers to the questions about my losses, I would get some peace of mind. My desire to make sense of a difficult and traumatic situation is not unique, by the way. To avoid stress or distress, humans attempt what scientists call "meaning-making" in a variety of ways, saying things like, "It's just one of those things," or "These things happen."[22]

Christians might try to make sense of a tragedy by applying the common (and often frustrating) platitude: "It must have been God's will."

A few people said this to me after my miscarriages, and frankly, I did not find that answer satisfactory or comforting. It was completely contrary to what I had read in the Bible of God's character; He is merciful, kind, and a loving parent, so what good could possibly come from letting my babies die?

Fast-forward to 2024, and I was smack-dab in the middle of writing this book when my women's Bible study leader chose for our summer reading Kristen LaValley's recent publication, *Even if He Doesn't: What We Believe about God When Life Doesn't Make Sense*. (God consistently amazes me with the timing of His love and grace!) Within the first few pages of LaValley's text, I was hit with this deep insight regarding my own search for answers in the midst of my grief:

> When something tragic happens, we try to make sense of it any way we can. We want to find a reason for it so we can escape it....When we're obsessed with finding the purpose for everything, we're seeking comfort in the purpose rather than the comfort of Christ.[23]

LaValley accurately expresses what I was doing throughout those four years of peppering God with questions after my miscarriages: I was seeking peace in the answers to my questions rather than seeking comfort in the Prince of Peace Himself. When I finally stopped asking God why these tragedies had happened and accepted the fact that the Lord, in His wisdom, was not going to tell me what I thought I needed to know, peace replaced frustration. When I reached this point of contentment with incomplete knowledge, the strangle-hold grief had on me began to loosen.

As you turn to the Lord in distress over your loss, feel free to make your complaint and ask your questions. Part and parcel with turning to God is asking Him if He is aware of your situation and why He is not showing Himself. The psalmists asked these very questions, and their reactions to tragedy are honest examples of how many of us feel when we are going through times of trouble today. What is important to realize in the structure of prayers of lamentation is that the Lord is not put off by our heartfelt inquiries.

He welcomes our questions because if we are seeking answers from Him, we are spending time in His presence. Questions lead to requests that lead to greater trust in Him that, in turn, leads to praise for His goodness and grace. But I am getting ahead of myself. Just remember that although the Lord may indeed provide us with answers at some point, obtaining these answers should not become our primary goal. Seek solace from your Heavenly Father, the "one who comforts the downcast," and trust that His comfort will be provided in the manner He deems most profitable for you.[24]

---

1. Acts 13:22.

2. Ps. 77:3, 6, KJV.

3. Strong, *Strong's Exhaustive Concordance*, under "H7878, *sîyach*."

4. *Collins Dictionary*, "complain," accessed June 14, 2024, https://www.collinsdictio nary.com/dictionary/english/complain: "to express resentment, displeasure, etc, esp habitually; grumble.

5. Strong, *Strong's Exhaustive Concordance*, under "H3885: *lûwn*: to be obstinate; to murmur"; "H8519: *telûnah*: in the sense of obstinacy; a grumbling, murmuring."

6. "For they did not believe in God and did not trust in His salvation" (Ps. 78:22).

7. Rothschild, "How Long O Lord?," 123.

8. Num. 14:28–29.

9. Eph. 4:26.

10. Vroegop, *Dark Clouds, Deep Mercy*, 32.

11. Remember that mercy is not simply a blessing; it is holding back from giving someone a punishment they deserve.

12. Job 1:8.

13. Job 3:3.

14. Job 37:19–20.

15. Job 9:16–17.

16. Job 38:4–7.

17. Job 42:3, 5.

18. 1 Chron. 16:4–7; Asaph wrote Pss. 50 and 73–83.

19. Ps. 73:3.

20. Ps. 73:21–24.

21. Ps. 102:2, NIV.

22. Park, "Religion as a Meaning-Making Framework," 708. Since the latter half of the twentieth century, psychologists have been studying human beings' propensity for "meaning-making," or the process by which humans use life experiences to build up knowledge that helps them make sense of how the world works. Humans experience stress or distress when the reality of new situations conflict with their expectations of how things should be. To relieve this distress, people attempt to attribute new meaning to their circumstances.

23. LaValley, *Even if He Doesn't*, 128, 23.

24. 2 Cor. 7:6.

Chapter Six

Request of the Lord

Do not forsake me, O Lord; O my God, be not far from me!
Make haste to help me, O Lord, my salvation!
Psalm 38:21–22

AMID THE BARRAGE OF questions to the Lord, I also made numerous requests of Him. I wanted to have more children, but as months turned into years, and my womb remained empty, I felt like Hannah, a "woman of sorrowful spirit," yearning for a child and pleading for the Lord to bless me with another baby.[1] Since I was missing an ovary and fallopian tube, I asked the Lord to make my remaining reproductive organs more effective. I requested strong eggs, a hospitable womb, good health, and the strength to carry the next baby full-term. With these very specific appeals, I was engaging in the third aspect of the lamentation process: making my requests known to God.

I want to pause here to make something abundantly clear: I was not asking the Lord to replace the children I had lost—that was not possible. My heart grieved the loss of two human beings who were exceptional and unique, and the birth of subsequent children could not make up for the loss of these two. I will, however, admit that becoming pregnant again became a priority after their loss.

There is nothing like the ache of empty arms after a miscarriage. Even if there are other children in the house, mothers have a deep understanding that one is missing, so the drive to have another baby after miscarriage is common and incredibly strong.

I have seen this desire in many women of my acquaintance as well as in most of the women I interviewed for this book. One hundred percent of the parents I interviewed continue to think of the babies they lost, and 80% wanted to get pregnant again as soon as they were able.[2] Forty percent think of their babies daily or a few times per week, 13.3% think of their babies 1–3 times per month, and 46.7% stated they mainly think of their babies on the expected due dates and on holidays.

Thus, grieving parents' desires for more children are not about getting "replacement" babies. As one of the mothers I interviewed explained, "Having another child will never replace your longing, love, and attachment to your loss." Having another child is instead about taking the love that had built up in the parents' hearts in anticipation of their deceased babies' births and getting the opportunity to express it to another tiny human.

How to Make Your Requests

The third step in the lamentation process is to make requests of the Lord (often pleas for help) during times of difficulty. However, when we are in pain, we may not be clear-sighted enough to recognize what we truly need, and this is why the structure of lamentation is so crucial. By first crying out to the Lord to vent our emotions and by explaining our problems to Him, we get a clearer perspective of our circumstances. Then as we spend time in our Father's presence, we will better understand His will for our lives, and our requests will be more likely to reflect His will than our own.

I want you to notice how, within numerous psalms, questions are quickly followed by the psalmists' requests for God's help. Using David again as our example, we can make comparisons between David's problems and the requests he makes of the Lord (see table 2). I'll admit that David is more eloquent in his expressions than most people tend to be, but within this poetry, David is clear about his condition and his needs: He is sinking under the oppression of his enemies and needs God's intervention and deliverance. David does not pull any punches. He needs help, he needs a particular kind of help, and he needs it now. Obviously, your requirements are quite different from David's (you probably don't need the Lord to smite your enemies), but you can still take a leaf out of the book of Psalms when it comes to your prayers.

Next, remember that you should not simply cry out for help, but you should be specific in the requests you make to the Lord. Spend some time pondering what you need in your current circumstances. What kind of help do you need? Do you need physical healing? Emotional healing? Relationship stability? Better doctors? Answers to medical questions?

Search your heart and consider your needs carefully. Be honest with yourself and seek the Lord's wisdom and understanding as you bring your requests to Him. Lamentation is almost like creating a mental spreadsheet that lays out each problem and identifies specific, God-centered solutions to these problems. Remember, we have a big God "who is able to do exceedingly abundantly above all that we ask or think," so be explicit with your requests.[3]

As a point of contrast with David's specific requests, let us look at an illustration of an ambiguous request. Imagine what would happen if you went out to dinner with some friends, and when the server approached your table to take your order, you simply said, "I'm hungry." The implication of these words is that you would like food of some sort, but how is the server to know what kind of food or how much? Would you be content with whatever the server decides to plop in front of you? Wouldn't you prefer to have a say in the selection?

I realize our Lord is omniscient and, therefore, already knows your likes and dislikes, and I also know that God knows best, but vagueness in our prayer life is a form of blindness. If we are not clear about our entreaties to Him, it is much more difficult for us to recognize when our prayers are answered. Direct answers to specific requests are far easier for us to identify as blessings from the Lord and harder to categorize as mere coincidences. (Think Gideon's fleece: Gideon's prayers were distinctive, and God answered them distinctively.) When there is no doubt that a specific prayer was answered by God, He gets the glory!

TABLE 2. David's Problems, Complaints, and Requests

David's Problem	David's Complaint	David's Request
His enemies are surrounding him, so he needs deliverance.	"Many are they who rise up against me" (Ps. 3:1).	"Arise, O Lord; save me, O my God! For you have struck all my enemies on the cheekbone; You have broken the teeth of the ungodly" (Ps. 3:7).
His enemies are trying to kill him, so he needs them to depart.	"They gather together, they hide, they mark my steps, when they lie in wait for my life" (Ps. 56:6).	"Put my tears into Your bottle. Are they not in Your Book? When I cry out to You, Then my enemies will turn back; this I know, because God is for me" (Ps. 56:8–9).
People are ridiculing him, so he needs the Lord's protection.	"But I am a worm, and no man; a reproach of men, and despised by the people" (Ps. 22:6). "I became a byword to them….And I am the song of the drunkards" (Ps. 69:11–12).	"But You, O Lord, do not be far from me; O my Strength, hasten to help me! Deliver me from the sword, my precious life from the power of the dog" (Ps. 22:19–20). "Let their table become a snare before them, and their well-being a trap. Let their eyes be darkened, so that they do not see" (Ps. 69:22–23).
He is afraid and wishes he could disappear to escape his pain.	"Fearfulness and trembling have come upon me, and horror has overwhelmed me. Oh, that I had wings like a dove! I would fly away and be at rest" (Ps. 55:5–6).	"Destroy, O Lord, and divide their tongues, for I have seen violence and strife in the city" (Ps. 55:9).
He is physically and emotionally exhausted from trying to escape his enemies.	"I am weary with my groaning; All night I make my bed swim; I drench my couch with my tears. My eye wastes away with grief" (Ps. 6:6–7).	"Let all my enemies be ashamed and greatly troubled; let them turn back and be ashamed suddenly" (Ps. 6:10).

Seeking God's Face in Supplication

Another thing to keep in mind when making your requests to the Lord is to differentiate between your wants and your needs. What we think we need during moments of crisis may not be the best thing for us. The more time you spend in the Lord's presence, the easier it will become to recognize the necessity of seeking God's will in your circumstances. He has a plan for your life, He knows what you need, and His timing of provision is best. For much of my life, I have heard many Christians reference Philippians 4:19 as a kind of "golden ticket" when they are asking for something of the Lord: "And my God shall supply all your need according to His riches in glory by Christ Jesus."

The problem with thinking of this scripture in such a way is that people fail to take into account what Paul was talking about in the previous eighteen verses. At the beginning of chapter four, Paul exhorts the brethren in Philippi not to be anxious about anything when they are praying and to present their requests to the Lord with *thanksgiving*. If they make their requests with a thankful heart, Paul promises in verse six that "the peace of God, which surpasses all understanding will guard your hearts and minds through Christ Jesus."

This is exactly what we need when we are in the depths of sorrow: peace that calms the turmoil in our hearts and in our minds—peace that comes from knowing that our God is in control: He sees us in our suffering, and He cares about and will take care of us in the midst of our suffering. Unfortunately, we sometimes get so focused on what is in God's hands that we fail to first seek His face.

Permit me another illustration. When my daughter and eldest son were about nine and eleven years old, I explained to them how our view of the Lord may become obstructed by our attention to things such as problems or desires. I sat the kids down on the couch and held a silver dollar between my thumb and forefinger about three feet from their faces. I asked them to focus on the coin and then asked if they could still see me okay. Their slowly drawn out, "Yeah…" hung in the air, accentuating their belief that Mom had finally cracked. Disregarding their confused expressions, I stepped forward, gradually inching the coin closer and closer to my son's nose. Every few seconds, I asked if he could still see me, and his answers of, "Yes...yes...yes," came less confidently the nearer I got to his face. When I was about five inches away, my son's eyes began to cross as he focused on the coin, and he said it was harder to see me. By the time I got two inches from his nose, he said he couldn't see me at all.

After repeating this process with my daughter, I explained the purpose of this object lesson: The coin was symbolic of our problems, and I represented our Heavenly Father who is waiting to help us in times of trouble. The more we concentrate our attention on our hardships, the more difficult it becomes to see the Lord even when He draws near to us. Although I was only about a foot and a half away from my kids by the end of the demonstration, their focus on the coin had completely obstructed their view of me.

How often do we let our problems or requests (which are often what we believe to be the solution to our problems) dominate our attention, preventing our ability to see and accept help from the One who "satisfies the longing soul and fills the hungry with goodness"?[4]

After my second miscarriage, I had allowed my sorrow to obstruct my view of God to the extent that the object of most of my attention was my own desires. I wanted a baby, and I wanted one immediately. I cried out to Him, I complained, I asked questions, and I requested that He bless us with more children, but I didn't move much past this approach. I prayed according to my wants, not God's will, and when my wants were not fulfilled as I desired, I got upset with God.

When I think of this now, I am ashamed that my hurts, my feelings, and my needs had become the object of my focus and prayers, especially when I compare my prayers to those of Jesus in the Garden of Gethsemane the night before He was crucified. Jesus knew what was coming; He saw the evidence of Roman cruelty lining the road each time He entered Jerusalem, including when He had arrived just a few days before. He knew that He would have to endure similar barbarism, take on the sin of the world, and as a result, be separated from His Heavenly Father. This knowledge created a level of stress and anguish we cannot begin to fathom, causing blood to pour from His skin as He prayed.[5]

Even as the blood dripped from His brow, our Lord's request had God at its center: "Father, if it is Your will, take this cup away from Me; nevertheless, not My will, but Yours, be done."[6] Jesus dreaded what was coming, and His prayer indicates that He held a sliver of hope that there would be some other way to cover the sins of humankind and bring us into relationship with our Heavenly Father. Nevertheless, Jesus yielded to His Father's will because Jesus understood God's sovereignty and wisdom.

Aligning Requests with the Will of the Lord

You may be wondering at this point in the process of lamentation if your requests of the Lord are in line with His will. Psalm 37:4 gives us a clue as to how to ensure proper alignment: "Delight yourself in the Lord, and he will give you the desires of your heart." People sometimes interpret this verse to mean if we really like the Lord, He will bless us with the things we want (thus, this verse's popularity as a refrigerator magnet), but let's perform a close reading of this scripture to see what is really going on here. Some of us have been taught that to "delight ourselves in the Lord" means to find satisfaction and joy in His presence, and this is definitely true. However, you may be surprised to learn that the Hebrew word translated as "delight" in this verse is 'ânag which means "to be soft, pliable, effeminate, or luxurious."[7]

This sheds light on a different interpretation of the first part of the verse. What if King David is saying that we must be soft and pliable in our dealings with the Lord? This could mean humbling ourselves and submitting to His will. 'Ânag may also indicate that when we submit ourselves to the Lord, we luxuriate in His presence. If this is the case, then the latter part of the verse probably doesn't mean that God will give us whatever our hearts desire. Rather, if we humble ourselves before the Lord, our desires will be more likely to line up with His. What God desires, we will desire. This is how building a relationship with the Lord works: When we spend time in His Word and in His presence, we learn about Him; His ways then become our ways, and we become more like Him.

Working through the pain of infant loss while striving to align human desires with the Lord's isn't always easy because grief is often messy, but fortunately for us, our Father has provided Psalm 119 to illustrate an effective method for seeking God's face in the midst of our pain. At 176 verses, Psalm 119 is the longest psalm, and another striking aspect of this psalm is the way its structure mimics the turbulent nature of grieving. Here are just a few examples of the psalmist's tug-of-war between his despair and acknowledgment that God's Word is a source of strength, comfort, hope, insight, and peace:

- "My soul melts from heaviness;
  Strengthen me according to Your Word" (verse 28).

- "This is my comfort in my affliction
  For Your Word has given me life" (verse 50).

- "My soul faints for Your salvation,
  But I hope in Your word" (verse 81).

- "Unless Your law had been my delight,
  I would then have perished in my affliction" (verse 92).

- "Consider my affliction and deliver me,
  For I do not forget Your law" (verse 153).

- "Let my cry come before You, O Lord;
  Give me understanding according to Your word" (verse 169).

Notice how this psalm perfectly demonstrates the continued surges of frustration and anguish. However, each time the waves of grief rise, the psalmist quells them by reiterating declarations of the power of God's Word. In fact, Psalm 119 contains two of the most famous of such declarations: "Thy word is a lamp to my feet and a light to my path," and "The entrance of Your words gives light; It gives understanding to the simple."[8]

The psalmist's response to trouble is a marvelous parallel to the way Jesus calmed the waves of the stormy Sea of Galilee in the fourth chapter of Mark. The moment the disciples cried for help, Jesus acted, and it took only three words from His mouth to meet their needs: "Peace, be still!" The moment these words left Jesus's mouth, the waves that had threatened to capsize the boat became motionless.[9]

So it is with the application of God's Word to our storms of life. As often as our sorrow looms menacingly overhead, we must call out to God, line up our requests with His Word, and then use Scripture to weather the storm and to regain the peace that passes all understanding—the peace that will sustain us.

Supplication Builds Relationship

Some of you may still be struggling with the idea of calling out to God and asking Him for help or material items, but I want you to remember something extremely important: This is all part of having a relationship with God. Have you ever wondered why He put humans on this earth to begin with? Human beings have wrestled with the "purpose of life" question for millennia, but the answer is truly quite simple: God designed and created human beings so we could fellowship with Him. (See Appendix E for an explanation of the gospel in a nutshell.) Part of relationship is communication, and part of communication is being honest about your feelings and needs.

If maintaining your relationship with God during this dark time feels like an uphill battle, know that prayers of lamentation have the potential to strengthen your relationship like nothing else can. Times of tribulation reveal to us just how inadequate we are to meet our own needs, and this often drives us to our knees in prayer.

A good friend of mine recently described how she got through a particularly difficult time in her life by talking with the Lord daily: "I would not like to go through that period of my life again, but the time I spent with the Lord was so precious. I got so much closer to Him because I spent a lot of time in prayer." Her faith grew stronger as her relationship with the Lord grew closer. She learned she could count on God and that He loved her. Know that the more often you pray, the more likely you are going to believe God cares about you, and the more you believe He cares, the more time you will continue to spend with Him.

The Word of God also emphasizes the importance and necessity of spending time with the Father when we are afflicted with hardship. James, the brother of Jesus, leaves no doubt as to our course of action during life's difficult seasons: "Is anyone among you suffering? Let him pray."[10] The Greek word for "pray" in this verse is *prŏsĕuchŏmai*, meaning, "to pray to God, supplicate, worship."[11] Note that this definition includes the act of worship as a part of the act of supplication. The reason for James's instruction to pray in this manner is provided in James 5:16: "The effective, fervent prayer of a righteous man avails much."[12] Note how James's description of prayers of suffering highlights not only the effort that is exerted, but it also emphasizes that we are active participants in conversations with God.

Prayer is not merely a requisition form we fill out and submit in expectation of the provision of goods or supplies. Prayer—and prayers of lamentation in particular—include supplication with a *worshipful focus on God*.

Remember that the Lord is ready and waiting for you to humbly take your requests to Him because He loves you, desires to meet your needs, and best knows how they should be met since He knows you better than anyone. In Psalm 139, David details the depth of God's knowledge of His children, reminding us that God is intimately "acquainted with all [our] ways."[13] There is nothing about you He does not know, including "the secrets of the heart"—the pain, confusion, and needs surrounding the loss of your baby.[14] Once you understand these facts, the process of lamentation will become easier because you will finally be honest with Him in your supplications and in expressing your desires.

The act of humbling yourself before your Heavenly Father as you make your requests to Him is an indication of trust—trust in His limitless power, His all-encompassing knowledge, and His love for you. Trust in the Lord is a natural result of remembering just who the Lord is.

This remembrance is often the *turning point* within mourning, and this, dear sister, is also the next step in the lamentation process.

---

1. 1 Sam. 1:15.

2. At the times of the interviews, miscarriages had occurred 1–34 years prior.

3. Eph. 3:20.

4. Ps. 107:9.

5. Uber et al., "Hematohidrosis: Insights in the Pathophysiology," e542. *Hematohidrosis* is a "spontaneous discharge of bloody secretion through intact skin or sweat glands."

6. Matt. 26:39, 42; Mark 14:36; Luke 22:42.

7. Strong, *Strong's Exhaustive Concordance*, under "H6026, 'ânag."

8. Ps. 119:105, 130.

9. Mark 4:39.

10. James 5:13.

11. Strong, *Strong's Exhaustive Concordance*, under "G4336, prŏsĕuchŏmai."

12. Strong, *Strong's Exhaustive Concordance*, under "G1754, ĕnĕrgĕō: to be active, efficient, effectual, fervent, and to be mighty in." The Greek word *ĕnĕrgĕō*, is translated as "effective, fervent" in this verse.

13. Ps. 139:3.

14. Ps. 44:21.

CHAPTER SEVEN

Turning Point: Remember the Lord

My flesh and my heart fail;
But God is the strength of my heart and my portion forever.
PSALM 73:26

SINCE "FAITH IS THE substance of things hoped for, the evidence of things not seen," then I must confess that for a couple of years after my miscarriages, my faith was at a very low ebb.[1] At that point in life, the evidence of things seen appeared to indicate to me that the Lord had removed His blessing over my little family. In the span of two years, we lost two babies as well as our small trucking business, and my husband and I were under physical, emotional, and financial stress. With the arrival of each menstrual cycle came a roller coaster of emotions; hope and expectancy were replaced by sadness, disappointment, and a slow solidification of the notion that the favor of the Lord seemed to be passing us by. Every month, my mood and my trust in the Lord's faithfulness took another hit.

Words of praise caught in my throat, and it took great physical effort to even part my lips in prayer. When words eventually trickled out, it seemed as though my prayers were going no further than the ceiling of my home. Make no mistake, I loved the Lord, but it became easier to let daily routines take priority over spending time alone with Him or studying His Word.

Around the third year of struggling with infertility, I became oh, so tired of being sad, and realization began to dawn that I had allowed my happiness to become dependent upon my circumstances. I acknowledged that, instead of working on my relationship with the Lord, I had been counting on another baby to make me happy again. As I write this text now, it is difficult for me to think about my state of mind for those three years because I am now keenly aware of how the enemy robbed my family and me. Not only did he steal two children from my womb, but he also stole from my other two children their once-cheerful mother. I was impatient, stressed, and not the mother I wanted to be. I was not so much living my life as surviving it.

One day, the Lord brought to my remembrance a verse someone had shared with me when I was going through a troubling time in high school: "You will show me the path of life; in Your presence is fullness of joy; at Your right hand, there are treasures forevermore."[2] Praise the Lord for His mercy! Despite my inclination toward self-pity and the blindness I'd allowed the enemy to impose upon me, God was gently guiding me back to His presence—the source of strength and true joy.

I had reached a turning point. I made the decision to rebuild my relationship with the Lord. God became the focus of my prayer life once again, and regular Bible reading reminded me of who my Heavenly Father is and what He has accomplished over the millennia. My trust in the Lord was reignited.

The Volta

Within the structure of songs and prayers of lamentation, there is also a turning point—a change in focus that has a direct impact on the poets' ability to trust in the Lord, and this turning point is a model for those of us in mourning. After the psalmists have cried out to the Lord and shared their complaints, their poetry shifts in tone. Literature scholars call this shift a *volta* (the Italian word for "turn"), and voltas are often identified by words such as "however," "but," or "yet."[3] Psalmists use voltas not just as a way of indicating a change in attitude but also to encourage readers to reflect upon what was said or what happened before the volta and to view that information in a new light.

Table 3 provides a breakdown of the elements of lamentation within Psalm 130 (a psalm of just eight verses) to give you an idea of how a volta functions in biblical poetry.

TABLE 3. Elements of Lamentation in Psalm 130

Element of Lamentation	Psalm 130 Verse
Cry out to the Lord.	[1] Out of the depths I cry to You, LORD.
Request of the Lord.	[2] Lord, hear my voice. Let Your ears be attentive to my cry for mercy.
Complain to and Question the Lord.	[3] If You, LORD, kept a record of sins, O Lord, who could stand?
Remember the Lord (Volta).	[4] But with You there is forgiveness, so that we can, with reverence, serve You. [5] I wait for the LORD, my whole being waits, and in His word I put my hope. [6] I wait for the Lord more than watchmen wait for the morning, more than watchmen wait for the morning.
Express Praise and Thanksgiving to the Lord.	[7] Israel, put your hope in the LORD, for with the LORD is unfailing love and with Him is full redemption. [8] He Himself will redeem Israel from all their sins.

Notice how the psalm begins with a sense of hopelessness as the psalmist cries out to the Lord, pleading for God to hear him. The reason for the poet's condition is expressed in verse three: "If you, LORD, kept a record of sins, Lord, who could stand?"[4] The psalmist knows his spiritual position is dire. However, in verse four, there is a volta—"But with You"—it's one tiny phrase, but it's one that carries a lot of weight because it precedes a great declaration of faith. In the midst of difficult circumstances, the psalmist makes a conscious effort to focus on God, His abilities, and His faithfulness.

Essentially, the volta within this psalm is the author's way of saying, "Hey! Check this out! I was in the depths of despair, but I now choose to hope and rejoice in my God because I can look at His track record, and I see that He is good—all the time!" Despair turns to reverence when the psalmist acknowledges that his God is greater than his own abilities or his circumstances. As he then waits upon and hopes in the Lord, he encourages all of Israel to do the same.

Let me pause here to give you a bit of advice: Avoid skipping over the psalms of lamentation. In the past, I tended to bypass what I thought of as the "weeping and wailing" parts of the Bible because I didn't think they really applied to me. (After all, I didn't live in a war zone, and I didn't have people out to get me or trying to kill me.) However, when we fail to read the verses of lament within the books of Psalms, Isaiah, Jeremiah, and Lamentations, we short-change ourselves. We miss out on the opportunity to see how overcoming trials hinges on a volta, a turn, an alteration of attitude that is enabled by remembering the faithfulness and character of our God.

While you are reading the Scriptures, look for the voltas in the psalms and prayers of lamentation, and you will notice how the psalmists' mindsets change when they remember the goodness of the Lord. Similarly, understanding the significance of a volta will bolster your faith when the enemy comes against you with the slings and arrows of life that threaten to pierce your heart in ways no natural weapon could:

> Who shall separate us from the love of Christ? Shall tribu-
> lation, or distress, or persecution, or famine, or nakedness,
> or peril, or sword? ... For I am persuaded that neither death
> nor life, nor angels nor principalities nor powers, nor things
> present nor things to come, nor height nor depth, nor any
> other created thing, shall be able to separate us from the love
> of God which is in Christ Jesus our Lord.[5]

Recognizing the volta in scripture may help you to view your circumstances through the lens of God's character and to learn that nothing the
enemy throws at you can separate you from the love of God.

Remember Who God Is

It is important to realize that the volta in lament results from remembering
who God is and what He has done, but as you grieve the loss of your
little one, there may be days when this will be a challenging task. I get
it. There were times during my mourning when it was difficult to recall
how my family and I had been blessed by the Lord in any way, shape, or
form. My mind was so absorbed by the duties and emotional turmoil of
life that remembrance of my Heavenly Father's goodness was often shoved
into the recesses of my brain. You may find yourself in a similar state of
mind on occasion. However, it is precisely during these demanding and
trying periods of life that you must be *intentional* about remembering the
goodness of your Heavenly Father.

By way of encouragement, let me give you a good starting point for this
step of lamentation: If you can remember nothing else that the Lord has done,
remember the cross. This is the easiest act of God to call to mind, and it truly
is the most important act of all. If the only words you are able to express are,
"Thank you, Father, for sending Jesus. Thank you, Jesus, for dying for my sins,"
you are well on your way to your volta. These words will remind you of your
Father's great love for you, His desire for relationship, and His provision of a

Savior. Once you remember these things, it becomes so much easier to trust Him with your pain and believe He can—and will—heal your broken heart.

Remembering God's character or nature is not a cliché; it is a necessary element of the process that helps pull you from the mire of grief. Taking the time to remember who God is will enable you to find safety and rest.

Exploring God's Character Through Bible Study

Spending time in God's Word is the best way for you to improve your understanding of His character, but since pain tends to direct people's focus inward, I'd like to recommend something to aid your Bible study process: Rather than looking in, look up. This piece of advice comes from Kristi McLelland, professor of biblical studies at Williamson College, who instructs her students to avoid reading the Bible through a Western lens (trying to to determine what God's Word teaches us about ourselves) and to instead read it through a Middle Eastern lens, a view that encourages one to ask, "What does it teach me about God?"[6] In other words, rather than reading the Bible as a way of finding out how God's Word relates to *you*, how it may improve *you*, or what it reveals about *you*, read the Bible as if it were a comprehensive course on *God*.

Changing the focus of Bible study from ourselves to the Lord brings greater revelation of His nature. For example, reading Psalm 23 through the Western lens is more likely to prompt us to make ourselves the central figure in this scenario by fixating on all the wonderful things our Shepherd does for *us*: We are not in want because He provides all our physical and spiritual needs, He keeps us safe, and He wants good things for us. In contrast, the Middle Eastern lens brings the *Shepherd's* character into clearer focus: He is a God who is caring, loving, regenerative, knowledgeable, strong, a safe haven, good, and merciful.

The Names of God

The Middle Eastern lens also helps you to gain greater understanding of your Heavenly Father's character when you study His various names. You may not be aware of it, but in the original Hebrew, God is known by numerous names that reveal different aspects of His nature. In most English translations of the Bible, however, the different names of God are translated simply as "God" or "Lord," titles which fail to indicate the particular attributes of God to which His people were appealing or that were on display at that moment in time. In her book *Praying the Names of God*, Ann Spangler explains that in antiquity, "names were often thought to reveal the essential nature and character of a person....To know God's name is to enjoy a kind of privileged access to him."[7] Simply put, knowing God's names helps you get to know Him better.

To illustrate this point, think about how the various names by which you are known reflect your intimacy levels with others. To get your attention as a child, family and friends probably called you by either your first or middle name, but if your parents used both these names together, you knew you were in trouble. If first, middle, and last names were used at once, heaven help you! Perhaps, rather than your given name, you're called by a nickname, one that tends to be reserved for those closest to you. You may also be called by any number of titles (e.g., Wife, Mom, Sister, Daughter, Teacher, Doctor, Nurse, Chef, or Housekeeper). Notice how the names others use for you indicate who you are as a person, your relationships, the closeness of these relationships, your capabilities, and the roles you fill.

Now consider how many more roles your Heavenly Father fills and the names you use to refer to Him. If your list is short ("God," "Lord," or "Father"), start paying attention to how and when God's names are used in Scripture. This may just open new levels of understanding regarding the power, strength, and abilities of the Lord. When you pray, choose the most appropriate name for the Lord in your supplications (see Appendix F for a list of the names of the Lord). Calling God by His various names will create an intimacy with Him you may not have experienced before, and intimacy fosters trust in the Lord who is the Mighty Creator, the Almighty, your Provider, Healer, Peace, Righteousness, and the Good Shepherd who meets your needs.

Praying the Names of God

Once you better understand the significance of God's names, it will become easier to use His names as you pray. Let's review Psalms 46 and 91 for a couple of examples of how you might apply this practice in your own prayer life. Despite the threat of chaos and imminent destruction, each of these songs begins by using the specific names of God that establish Him as the Almighty, Most High God to make a declaration of His authority, strength, and protection (see table 4).

TABLE 4. Using God's Names in Declarations of Trust (Psalms 46 and 91)

Psalm	Problem	Names of God Used in Psalm	Opening Declaration
Psalm 46	Waters roar, mountains shake, nations rage, and kingdoms are moved.	Elohim (God, Mighty Creator); 'El·Elyōn (Most High)	"God is our refuge and strength, A very present help in trouble. Therefore we will not fear" (vv. 1 and 2).
Psalm 91	Perils, pestilence, and traps abound; thousands are dying left and right.	Yahweh (LORD); 'El·Elyōn (Most High)	"I will say of the LORD, 'He is my refuge and my fortress; My God, in Him I will trust'" (v. 2).

You may be wondering how these psalmists reached such astounding levels of trust in the Lord in the midst of difficult circumstances, and the answers are found in two key verses. In the first verse, Psalm 46:10, the Lord says, "Be still and know that I am God; I will be exalted among the nations, I will be exalted in the earth!" Remember that being "still" is more than simply shutting yourself off from the craziness of the world and being quiet in God's presence. Rather, it is taking shelter in Him, much like one would in the tower of a fortress. While nestled in this position of security, we will have a front-row seat to His exaltation and glorification. This is intimacy. This is what it means to *know that He is God*. What a privilege!

The second scripture, Psalm 91:14, explains that an important part of cultivating a relationship with God is knowing Him by name. Here, the psalmist declares, "Because he has set his love upon Me, therefore I will deliver him; I will set him on high, because he has known My name." The Hebrew word for "known" in this verse, *yâda'*, has numerous meanings, including, "to know, to ascertain by seeing; recognition; familiar with (as with a friend); and to regard or have respect for."[8] Therefore, the implication of this verse is not that God exalts those who happen to know what His various names are. (After all, anybody can know what His names are. Even the devil knows what God's names are.) No, in Psalm 91:14, the Lord is describing an intimate relationship wherein His child loves and respects his Father not simply for what He can do but because *he knows who He is.*

When you declare the names of the Lord in your prayers of lamentation, you remind yourself (and your enemy) exactly who God is, what He is able to do in any given situation, and the level of intimacy you have with Him. The result of having the Psalm 91:14 type of relationship with the Lord is your deliverance from sin, this world, and all its troubles; it is an exaltation to the status of a Child of God. It is restoration. It is love.

Remember What God Has Done: Ebenezers

When we remember and acknowledge who God is, we are better equipped to recognize His mighty hand at work, but our Heavenly Father wants us to go beyond mere recognition of His handiwork. God expects us—indeed, He commands us—to *remember* what He has done for us. It is one thing to acknowledge God did something in our lives. It is another thing to remember, down the road, what He did in the past.

As a point of comparison, think about how many birthday presents you can remember receiving over the years. Do you remember what your spouse or friend gave you just last year? The year before? The year before that? I would venture a guess that the gifts you remember best are the ones you found special at the time, and these are the gifts you display, wear, or use most often. When you do so, you think of and are grateful for the giver as well as the gift.

God does not want you to remember the things He has done for you or the blessings He has given you just so you can say, "Wow, Lord! What a cool present!" He wants you to remember His actions as a reflection of who He is to you: a good and faithful God and Father. To give you a better sense of the importance God places on our remembrance of His acts, permit me another word study. The Hebrew words for "remember" (*zâkar*) and "remembrance" (*zeker*) are used 256 times in the Bible, referring to times when both God and human beings remembered things.[9]

When God "remembers" something, however, this is not an indication that someone or something was simply called to mind; the Lord's "remembrance" of people or His covenants with them is always followed by another action on His part. For example, when God remembers Noah after the flood, He sends winds to dry the waters, and He sets the rainbow in the sky as evidence of His covenant. When God remembers His covenant with Abraham, He spares Lot's life from the destruction of Sodom and Gomorrah. When God remembers Rachel and Hannah, He "open[s] their wombs" so they can bear children. When He hears the cries of the Israelites in Egypt, God remembers His Abrahamic covenant and sends Moses to deliver them from bondage.[10] God's remembrance of this covenant is also what brought back Jews from around the globe to their homeland and enabled the state of Israel to be reestablished in 1948.[11]

When humans in the Bible "remember" something the Lord did for them, they respond by establishing memorials of how the Lord met their needs:

- After the Lord provided a ram as a replacement when Abraham was about to sacrifice Isaac, Abraham paid tribute to this event and named the place, "The Lord will provide."[12]

- After the Children of Israel crossed the Jordan River into the Promised Land, Joshua built a twelve-stone memorial in the midst of the Jordan and another monument of twelve stones at Gilgal as a reminder that the Israelites and the ark of the covenant crossed over on dry ground.[13]

- The Law of Moses required the Israelites to add tassels to their clothing so that every time they looked at the tassels, they would "remember and do all [Gods'] commandments, and be holy unto [their] God."[14]

- To commemorate the Lord's deliverance of His people from the Philistines, Samuel set up a stone memorial, calling it an *Ebenezer*, meaning, "Thus far the Lord has helped us."[15]

Each of these "Ebenezers," or memorials, was intended to be a reminder of a miraculous or pivotal event experienced by God's people. The purpose for these tributes was not only to glorify God, but they were also designed to prevent people from forgetting what their God had done for them.

It may seem an obvious point that a memorial helps people remember a significant event or person, but how often does the memory of the marvelous things God has done in our lives fade with time? When life gets busy, how often do we intentionally—and without prompting—recall the ways in which God has blessed us over the years?

When I get frustrated or discouraged while waiting for answers to prayer, or when the enemy whispers in my ear that God doesn't care about me or my circumstances, I remember my own little Ebenezer: the bead in the carpet.

The Bead in the Carpet

In the early 2000s, lampshades with dangly beads were quite the decorating trend, and after several months' yearning, I finally obtained a floor lamp and a table lamp with antique gold stands and white lampshades which stood in pride of place near my sofa. Each lampshade was adorned with numerous strands of beads on the bottom edge, and each strand contained at least ten, tiny, round, beads with one teardrop shaped bead at the end. (Please refrain from any judgment. You know darn well that 10-20 years from now, your progeny are going to laugh just as hard at pictures of your farmhouse décor, but I digress...)

One day when my children were 11, 9, 4, and 2 years old, motherhood for me had essentially been a lesson in herding cats. I don't remember the exact circumstances of that day; I just remember my husband was working another twelve-hour shift, my kids were all needing something at once (meaning simultaneously and immediately), and I was exhausted.

At some point, I looked up from speaking with one of my children and noticed my two-year-old perched on the arm of the couch, reaching for the beads of the floor lamp. His arm was stretched to the maximum as he wriggled his chubby fingers amongst the beads.

"Patrick! *NO!*" I bellowed from across the room.

Alas! The beads were too enticing, and just as I bolted toward him, my toddler's hand closed into a fist around two strands. Before I could reach him, he yanked, and a couple dozen of the tiny beads cascaded onto the carpet below. Picking up my son, I pried open his fist to retrieve only about five beads, and I handed him to my daughter with a flustered, "Take your little brothers to their room, so I can clean up this mess."

Although this description of my reaction may sound fairly rational and tame, I assure you, in reality, it was anything but. As soon as the kids were out of the room, I became a woman obsessed.

"My lamp!" I wailed. "My lamp! It's ruined! Can't we have *anything* nice in this house?"

After a hasty comparison of the remaining strands of beads on the lampshade to the bare strings that now mocked me in their nakedness, I calculated just how many beads were missing. I began rummaging through the carpet, ply by ply, seeking taupe-colored beads that (I had not realized until that moment) were a perfect color-match to the carpet. It was worse than trying to find a needle in a haystack—needles at least contrast with hay in their color and luster.

Several minutes of searching revealed that one bead was still missing. It might not seem like a big deal, but at that moment, that one, tiny bead seemed to symbolize the chaos of my life. The desperation of my search became absurd. Crumbling to the floor near the lamp, I leaned my head against the wall and began to pray through my tears: "Lord, I know this is a stupid request, but would You please show me where that last bead is? I just want my lamp to look pretty again."

Feeling terribly sorry for myself, I sat, staring at the ceiling for a few moments. Then with a heavy sigh, I resumed my search, separating the strands of carpet for the hundredth time. A gasp of amazement escaped my lips as I spied the bead lying atop the carpet's hard, ivory backing. With the bead gently cradled in the palm of my hand as fresh tears blurred it from view, I whispered to the Lord, "You care! You really care!"

This knowledge was a revelation to me then, and the story of that bead is a precious reminder to me now that the Lord is mindful of every aspect of my life. He cares about everything—the major things, the difficult things, and even those things that may seem mundane or trivial. He truly cares. He even cares about a bead in a carpet.

Your Ebenezer

Here is the kicker, my dear sister: If God cares about these little things, He cares about the great things, the wonderful things, the painful things, and the heartbreaking things in life, including the loss of your child. I challenge you to ponder what your own Ebenezer might be. Examine your life, and remember those times when the Lord showed up, when He helped you, when He delivered you, when He answered your prayers, and when He provided for your needs. Create an Ebenezer in your home or yard. It may be a picture, a trinket, a precious memento, or a stack of stones, but select something that will be within view on a regular basis to remind you of the Lord's faithfulness in the past.

When you produce a monument that commemorates your God, you will be reminded of His character, actions, abilities, and faithfulness each time you look at it, and this is especially necessary while you are grieving your loss and when discouragement threatens to obstruct your view of who God truly is:

> The Ebenezers in our lives are stationary reminders, but when
> we remember them, we don't stay still. We move toward hope.
> We step into joy. We respond to what's true. If God was faithful

then, he is faithful now. And if he's faithful now, he'll be faithful
in the future too.[16]

Instead of allowing the challenges of life to create distance between you and
the Lord, Ebenezers will remind you to lean into the One who has been there
for you before and who will be there for you again.

The structure of lamentation encourages you to remember the Lord's character
and to review the record of His actions and faithfulness as a means of gently
guiding you to the point of trusting the Lord, and learning to trust Him is key
to processing grief. To trust the Lord means to have a "firm belief in the reliability, truth, or ability of" your Heavenly Father.[17] Implementing the process
of lamentation when you are mourning the loss of your little one will help you
to trust in the Lord's reliability, truthfulness, and abilities no matter what your
eyes see:

> Trust is believing what you know to be true even though the
> facts of suffering might call that belief into question. Lament
> keeps us turning toward trust by giving us language to step
> into the wilderness between our painful reality and our hopeful
> longings.[18]

What a marvelous gift is lamentation! It is a godly way of communicating
with the very One—the only One—who can buoy your faith when you feel you
are drowning in grief. When you truly understand who God is, what He has
done, and what He will continue to do, you will then be given the language to
praise the Lord.

1. Heb. 11:1.

2. Ps. 16:11.

3. "Volta," Poets.org, accessed July 20, 2024, https://poets.org/glossary/volta. "Volta" is also called "turn, fulcrum, or hinge." This term was originally applied to sixteenth century Italian sonnets and later applied to Shakespearian sonnets to describe a dramatic change of content or tone between stanzas.

4. Strong's, *Strong's Exhaustive Concordance*, "H5975, *'âmad*"; "Benson Commentary, Psalm 130," Bible Hub., accessed September 3, 2024. https://Biblehub.com/com mentaries/benson/psalms/130.htm. The Hebrew word for "stand" in this verse is *'âmad* which, in addition to meaning "abide or stand fast," is also a judicial phrase, referring to "a man being absolved or justified upon a fair trial." Thus, the psalmist's question indicates his awareness that if he were to stand trial in the court of the Lord on Judgment Day, he would lose his case: He would be found guilty of sin, would have no way of absolving himself of sin, and would therefore be banished from the presence of the Lord. It is easy to understand his desperation when we consider we all stand in these same shoes.

5. Rom. 8:35–39.

6. McLelland, *Jesus and Women*, 14.

7. Spangler, *Praying the Names of God*, 11.

8. Strong, *Strong's Exhaustive Concordance*, under "H3045, *yâda'*."

9. Strong, *Strong's Exhaustive Concordance*, under "H2142, *zâkar*: to mark; to remember; keep in remembrance; be mindful of." *Zâkar* (usually translated as "remember") is used 233 times throughout the Bible. *Zéker* (translated as "memorial" or "remembrance") is used 23 times.

10. Gen. 8:1; Gen. 9:15–16; Gen. 19:29; Gen. 30:22; 1 Sam. 1:19; Exod. 6:5.

11. See the books of Isaiah, Jeremiah, and Ezekiel for prophesies regarding this event.

12. Gen. 22:14.

13. Josh. 4:7.

14. Num. 15:39–40.

15. 1 Sam. 7:12.

16. LaValley, *Even if He Doesn't*, 90.

17. *Oxford English Dictionary*, under "trust."

18. Vroegop, *Dark Clouds, Deep Mercy*, 77.

CHAPTER EIGHT

Praise the Lord

Great is the Lord and most worthy of praise;
His greatness no one can fathom.
PSALM 145:3, NIV

"YOU NEED TO GET into praise."

A few months after the second miscarriage, my family and I had popped by my in-laws' house for a visit. Alone with me in the kitchen, my mother-in-law had just asked how I was doing, but when my response came too slowly, she looked me over with a knowing eye and said, "You need to get into praise."

As my eyes bored into hers, she laid her hand on my arm and emphatically advised: "Turn on some worship music and praise the Lord."

My mother and father-in-law, Lennie and Roger, are remarkable people who have faithfully served the Lord as pastors, teachers, and mentors for several decades. They have seen God perform many miracles at numerous times and in numerous ways during those so-called "mountaintop" moments of walking with the Lord, but they have also experienced His equally miraculous love as He supported them through life's darkest valleys. As I've mentioned in previous chapters, the Lord was there for them when their three-month-old daughter died from pneumonia, and God also helped them navigate grief twelve years later when their sixteen-year-old son died in an automobile accident.

Therefore, when Lennie told me that spending time praising the Lord would help me process my grief, I knew she wasn't just spouting a platitude to ease the discomfort of the moment. I knew she had the experience to support what she was telling me to do. I knew she understood (better than any mother should) what it felt like to lose children. I knew in my head Lennie's advice was sound. I knew all these things, but the problem was, my heart rebelled against the idea of praise.

After Lennie finished speaking, I nodded my head and pursed my lips together to prevent them from expressing what I was thinking.

Praise the Lord? I questioned silently. *I really don't have the energy to sing praises—and if I'm honest, I really don't feel like praising the Lord.*

At that point, I had been walking in a fog of sadness for nearly two years. I passed through the doors of our church feeling like I didn't belong there anymore. I absolutely loved the Lord, but I didn't feel the joy of the Lord. I attempted to smile at others and tried to say all the right things, but my heart wasn't in it. There were many Sundays when I barely mouthed the words of the praise and worship music because it seemed disingenuous to sing what I didn't feel.

As I sit here now with my armchair quarterback's helmet figuratively strapped to my head, I am better able to determine the root of the problem I had with praise at that point in my life: I believed my ability to praise the Lord was grounded in *emotion* rather than a recognition and acknowledgment of who God is.

How I wish I had known then what I know now about how the lamentation process guides one into the ability to praise. If I had understood the power and effects of praise while in the depths of my grief, I would not only have been better able to weather life's tragedies themselves, I would have had joy more abundantly in the aftermath—during those long days that followed the storms when my new normal had two large holes that I had no power to fill; those days of waiting to hear from my Heavenly Father who seemed to have gone strangely quiet; those days of waiting for peace, for comfort, for understanding, for answers.

I would have had joy in the waiting because lamentation would have directed me to keep turning to the Lord, remembering His faithfulness, trusting in Him no matter what I saw, and praising Him throughout it all.

The Lord's Provision to Those in Mourning

At this point in your grieving process, you may also be finding it challenging to praise the Lord because vocalizing praise can be one of the hardest things to do when a person is in pain. Praise may also be difficult when you don't understand how praise is physically possible or what it can accomplish spiritually. However, let me offer a bit of good news. You have a merciful and gracious Heavenly Father who has ensured that you don't have to go through this last step of the lamentation process unaided. Your God is Jehovah Jireh. He is your provider, and just as the Lord provides in every other aspect of your life, He is there to give you the help and the strength you need to offer praise to Him while yet in sorrow.

To learn about Jesus's method for helping His brokenhearted children regain their ability to praise the Lord, follow me to a small synagogue in Nazareth. It is a Sabbath day, circa 30 AD, and Jesus steps forward to read from the scrolls of scripture. He selects the opening verses of Isaiah 61 (a psalm of lamentation), but instead of expounding upon the chapter as is traditional for rabbis, Jesus declares, "Today, this scripture has been fulfilled in your hearing."[1] Disciples from the first to twenty-first century recognize this statement as Jesus's declaration that He is the Christ, but I want you to pay close attention to the way Jesus kicks off His ministry.

By highlighting this chapter of Isaiah, Jesus is doing more than proclaiming His identity; He is also pointing to God's provisions for those held captive by sin and for those who mourn. Examine the wording in the first three verses of

Isaiah 61 and notice Christ's emphasis on *how* He will minister to the needs of those with broken hearts:

> The Spirit of the Lord is upon Me,
> Because the Lord has anointed me
> To preach good tidings to the poor in spirit;
> He has sent Me to heal the brokenhearted,
> To proclaim liberty to the captives ...
> To comfort all who mourn,
> To console those who mourn in Zion,
> To give them beauty for ashes,
> The oil of joy for mourning,
> The garment of praise [*tehillâh*] for the spirit of heaviness.[2]

These scriptures conveniently list just how the Lord goes about healing the brokenhearted, beginning with His promise to "comfort all who mourn." In this passage, the prophet Isaiah is speaking to the small remnant of Jews who remained in Israel, grieving for those who were forced into exile or taken into Babylonian captivity. Although you cannot truly relate to the grief of exile felt by these Jews, when you are mourning infant loss, you may also experience a sense of banishment from the life you once knew—a feeling of stagnation and separation while the rest of the world goes about its business, seemingly unaffected by your loss. The Lord brings comfort and consolation to you by drawing you home from exile to live with your King in a dwelling place where you are seen, valued, and loved.

After consolation, the Lord promises to give you "beauty for ashes." If this sounds strange to your ear, it may help to know that in ancient times, the Children of Israel would sprinkle ashes on their heads as an outward indication of mourning. Therefore, what is illustrated in Isaiah 61:3 is the Lord's washing away of the ashes of mourning and replacing them with "beauty," or *pe'êr*, a Hebrew word used only seven times in the Old Testament, and "pe'êr" doesn't merely mean something that is pretty. This word refers to the ornaments worn by a bride or to the turban worn by priests who entered the holiest of holies in the Tabernacle.[3] Simply put, in exchange for the residue of death and sorrow, the Lord sets upon your brow a headdress of honor and dignity that is symbolic of intimacy with Him.

Once this coronation takes place, the Lord anoints you with the "oil of joy." In Hebrew culture, oil is an important substance that has multiple functions. It is used for food and fuel, and because oil is "regarded as a symbol of honor, joy, and favor," it is also reserved for use in the anointing process.[4] Unfortunately, because of oil's symbolism, ancient Jews refrained from anointing themselves while they were in mourning (an indication of profoundness of their sorrow), and/or if they had been in contact with someone deceased.[5] However, Isaiah's prophesy reveals the Messiah's plan to turn this practice around.

Jesus ensures that the bereaved are not simply included in the anointing process, He provides a special oil just for them. Christ's application of the "oil of joy" removes the stigma associated with death and sorrow and replaces it with honor, favor, and reconciliation with Him. This is possible because the oil is not made of crushed olives or some other earthly element. This oil consists of joy—joy that is not a mere emotion but is an outward expression of exultation and celebration irrespective of circumstances.[6] This is the same kind of joy felt by the magi upon seeing the star that led them to the Christ child, the joy which is the reward of the "good and faithful servant" in Jesus's parable of the talents, and the joy the women at the tomb experienced after the angel of the Lord told them that Jesus was alive and not dead.[7] This very same joy is the substance the Lord uses to anoint your mourning when you place yourself in His care.

Finally, after all these things, the Lord lays upon your shoulders the "garment of praise." I picture this garment as something similar to the Robe Royal that adorns monarchs' shoulders at their coronations. (You know, the purple, velvet robe trimmed with white fur?) However, this robe isn't for looks or prestige; it is a garment designed to cloak you in the Lord's presence where you can "be still and know He is God."[8] It is here where your state of grief and depression ("the spirit of heaviness") is exchanged for the strength and ability to praise the King of kings.

Dear sister, please realize that healing your broken heart and getting you through the lamentation process to the point of being able to praise the Lord is in your Savior's job description. Scripture tells us again and again that your Heavenly Father's eyes are upon you, He hears your cries, and He cares for you.[9] He knows you need to weep and to grieve, and the Lord is not expecting you to praise Him while you are still sitting at your baby's graveside, covered in the ashes of sorrow.[10] When you, God's child, turn to the Lord in your grief, the Lord paves the way to praise: He restores you from exile, welcomes you into His arms, sets a crown upon your head, anoints you with joy, and adorns you with the garment of praise. This is what makes it possible for you to worship the Lord in the midst of heartache.

A Song in the Night

Despite having the strength and ability to praise, there will be times when singing while you are choking on the lump in your throat will seem impossible. Don't worry! The Lord has prepared for this eventuality as well. He knows grief is cyclical. He knows there will be days when you are able to resume regular activities and accomplish tasks much like before, but He also knows that there will be times when sleep eludes you, when darkness engulfs you, when you soak your pillow with tears, and when every muscle in your body aches from crying. Therefore, when grief overwhelms you with its paralyzing power in both figurative and literal darkness, know that the Lord has made another provision for you: His song in the night.

The Song of Asaph

Scripture illustrates how songs in the night are provided by the Lord to redirect our focus from our circumstances to Him, prompting us to remember who He is, what He has done, and what He can do. For example, Asaph begins Psalm 77 by crying out and complaining to the Lord, but then in verse six, he says, "I call to remembrance *my song in the night*; I meditate within my heart, and my spirit makes diligent search" (emphasis added). Asaph's "search" entails a review of his questions about the faithfulness of his God (i.e., "Will the Lord cast off forever? And will He be favorable no more?").[11] After admitting that dwelling on these questions brings him misery, Asaph makes a conscious decision to remember times when his Lord was faithful and spends the remainder of the psalm extolling the majesty of God.[12]

Because it enables Asaph to ask and answer very human questions about God's faithfulness, this song in the night is the turning point (volta) in the psalmist's grief process. Psalm 77 is not just a lamentation; it is a lesson in how to respond to doubts about God's character.

A Song in Prison

Paul and Silas's prison hymns are another powerful illustration of the effects of songs in the night.[13] Although you may already be familiar with this tale, allow me to provide additional context. Paul and Silas were brought up on trumped-up charges and received punishments that were excessive, cruel, and illegal.[14] Keep in mind that Roman forms of corporal punishment were brutal and intended to publicly humiliate as well as to physically harm their victims. Both men were likely stripped naked before being beaten with rods of either metal or iron until their ribs were broken and the flesh on their backs ripped open. Then, bleeding and utterly exhausted, they were thrown into prison.

At midnight, something extraordinary was heard from deep within the inky darkness of the prison. Two reedy voices cut through the stillness that had only been broken before by muffled moans or the clanking of prison inmates' metal chains. Paul and Silas's songs may have begun in low whispers, but as the minutes ticked by and their focus was directed more upon God than on the wounds on their backs, the Bible says the volume of their hymns rose until everyone in the prison could hear their praises to the Lord.

Consider the magnitude of this moment. If you were in the position of Paul and Silas and had endured excruciating torture, would you be physically or mentally able to open your mouth to sing? They were only human, so how did they do it? What enabled them to praise the Lord under such conditions? The Author and Finisher of their faith must be the answer to these questions.[15] From within the walls of a Roman prison, the Lord provided them with "songs in the night"—not merely the music and lyrics but the *physical ability* to sing as well.

The marvelous thing about this story is that Paul and Silas's songs of praise prompted an earthquake that opened the prison doors, loosened everyone's chains, and led to the salvation of the prison guard and his entire household![16] Ponder this for a moment. Praise made a way out of bondage—not only for the two men who sang but for many other people as well. Therefore, if praise were able to make a way out of literal bondage for all these people, imagine how praise will work to break the chains of grief wrapped around your heart.

Types of Praise

Not only does the Bible explain that the Lord *makes it possible* for us to praise Him, but God's Word also conveniently supplies us with numerous examples of the *methods* we can use to do so. First of all, you should know that praise is more than singing songs in a church service or thanking God for something He has done. Praise is an expression of honor or adoration, and praising God means you are glorifying Him, or "bestowing honor, praise, or admiration."[17] I was surprised to learn that in English Bibles, the word "praise" was actually translated from no fewer than nineteen different Hebrew and Greek words that each have very distinct meanings.[18]

Don't panic, I won't expound upon every form here, but I have provided a snapshot of the most common types of praise used specifically in songs and poems of lamentation as examples of how to praise the Lord while in mourning (see Appendix G). When the children of God praised the Lord in their sorrow, they bowed, knelt, or prostrated themselves before the Lord; they raised their hands or extended their arms; they spoke, shouted, or sang their praise; they worshipped publicly and privately. Bottom line: they were expressive in their praise of the Lord, and they didn't limit themselves to a single form of praise because each style served a different purpose. (If you are up to it, you can review the effects of the various types of praise in Appendix H: "A Deeper Dive into Praise.")

Praising the Lord: Where to Begin

At this point in your lamentation process, you may be eager to move on to the final step and begin praising the Lord, or you may feel that all this information on praise may seem good in theory, but you may be unsure about how to put it into practice.

A good place to start is to review the various types of praise in Appendix G and then select one or a few that interest you. Next, find yourself a peaceful place (away from people and electronic devices) and praise the Lord in your style of choice. Kneel before the Lord. Lie on your face before Him. Raise your hands. Raise your voice. The Lord likes every style of praise, and I assure you, He's not going to be picky about your method or the sound of your voice. The main thing is to make praise a regular part of your life, and the more you practice praise, the more it will become second nature.

If you are struggling to find words or songs of praise in this final step of lamentation, I have a few recommendations. Listen to Christian music on the radio or a streaming service and play this music in your car or home as you go about your daily activities. Try different genres, such as contemporary/pop, gospel, or rap, and don't disqualify the old-time hymns—their lyrics are truly captivating. Find songs from when you first became a Christian or from your teens. (Believe me, your generation is not unique in thinking you had the greatest music of all time, and there is something uplifting about listening to the songs of your youth.)

I also encourage you to pore over David's songs when you are seeking ways to praise the Lord. Flip through the pages of the book of Psalms, and you may be surprised at how many of them you already know because you've sung them at church in the past. Speak the words. Sing them. Allow the lyrics of the master psalmist to fill your mouth and to ascend as a sweet-smelling sacrifice of praise to the Lord.

One of my favorite psalms of praise is Psalm 3 because it always inspires me whenever the cares of life become too heavy. Even if I can only manage a murmur at first, David's lyrics provide comfort and peace during dark days and nights:

> But You, O Lord, are a shield for me,
> My glory and the One who lifts up my head.
> I cried to the Lord with my voice,
> And He heard me from His holy hill. *Selah*
> I lay down and slept;
> I awoke, for the Lord sustained me.[19]

Only our Heavenly Father can fully and truly transform the aspect of grief into a posture of joy. As I sing the words of this psalm, I can almost feel the Lord's finger under my chin, lifting my face heavenward. God is indeed the lifter of my head, for He protects me, honors me, hears me, refreshes me, and helps me to rest. I therefore encourage you to speak or sing the words of this psalm and experience the change that will take place when you shift your focus from your sorrow to the Lord: The weight of grief will be lifted from your shoulders as your Heavenly Father comforts you, restores your strength, and brings you peace.

---

1. Luke 4:21.

2. Isa. 61:1, 3; Strong, *Strong's Exhaustive Concordance*, under "H8416, *tehillâh:* a song of praise, adoration, glory."

3. Strong, *Strong's Exhaustive Concordance*, under "H6287, *pe'êr:* an embellishment; a fancy head dress." Exod. 39:28; Isa. 3:20; Isa. 61:3; Isa. 61:10; Ezek. 24:17; Ezek. 24:23; and Ezek. 44:18.

4. Gruber and Rabinowitz, "Oils," 395-396, accessed October 1, 2025. (See also Judg. 9:9, Ps. 45:8, Deut. 33:24, and Ps. 23:5.)

5. Being around deceased persons rendered mourners "ritually impure," requiring their purification and separation from others (Lev. 21:11–22; 2 Sam. 14:2; Dan. 10:3).

6. Strong, *Strong's Exhaustive Concordance*, under "H8342, *sason*."

7. Matt. 2:10; Matt. 25:21; Matt. 28:8. Strong, *Strong's Exhaustive Concordance*, under "G5479, *chara*: joy, rejoicing"; "Chara" is the Greek equivalent to the Hebrew word, "sason."

8. Ps. 46:10.

9. Ps. 33:18; Prov. 15:3; 1 Pet. 3:12.

10. John 11:35, 38.

11. Ps. 77:7–9.

12. Ps. 77:10.

13. Strong, *Strong's Exhaustive Concordance*, under "G5214, *humneō*: to sing a religious ode; to celebrate God in song."

14. Robinson, *Penal Practice and Penal Policy in Ancient Rome*. Roman citizens were not permitted to be beaten, flogged, or crucified except in extreme cases such as treason. However, Paul ultimately endured all of these punishments (2 Cor. 11:23–27). The magistrates are terrified of being punished themselves for inflicting this punishment on Paul and Silas once they hear that the men are actually Roman (Acts 16:37–40).

15. Heb. 12:2.

16. Acts 16:25–32.

17. *Merriam-Webster Dictionary Online*, "Praise," last updated January 21, 2025, https://www.merriam-webster.com/dictionary/praise; Ibid, "Glorify," last updated January 30, 2025, https://www.merriam-webster.com/dictionary/glorify.

18. For a list of the words translated as "praise" along with the numerical designations and definitions supplied by James Strong's *Strong's Exhaustive Concordance*, see Appendix G.

19. Ps. 3:3–5.

CHAPTER NINE

The Impacts of Praise

O Lord, You are my God.
I will exalt You,
I will praise Your name,
For You have done wonderful things;
Your counsels of old are faithfulness and truth.
Isaiah 25:1

MY ELDEST SON, SPENCER, was a very active child who loved playing outside and ran more than he walked. One fall morning when he was about two years old, we went to the park, and he dragged me by the hand straight to the "big kids" slide. Despite my protests that this slide was too high, he was adamant, so after helping him climb to the top, I stood at the foot, cheering him on and readying myself to catch him. Unfortunately, this slide lived up to the very name of slide, and before I knew it, my son had whizzed past my waiting arms and face-planted in the groundcover at my feet. I didn't wait for the tears that I knew were on the way but quickly scooped him up and held him tight against my chest, knowing what my child required before he could even cry out: security and comfort.

The Shadow of His Wings

When your heart is aching and longing for your little one, remember that your Heavenly Father knows what you need even before you ask, and it is His desire to hold you close and give you consolation. Because we cannot physically fall into the Lord's arms while we are on this earth, He has provided a spiritual haven for us that is accessible through the act of praise. The Word of God calls this special dwelling place, "the shadow of the Almighty," and in the numerous biblical references to the "shade" or "shadow" of the Lord, God's shadow is revealed to be a place of healing and protection.[1] Here are just a few examples:

- "He who dwells in the secret place of the Most High / Shall abide under *the shadow of the Almighty*" (Ps. 91:1).

- "Keep me as the apple of Your eye; / Hide me under *the shadow of your wings*" (Ps. 17:8).

- "How precious is your loving kindness, O God! / Therefore, the children of men put their trust under *the shadow of Your wings*" (Ps. 36:7).

- "Because You have been my help, / Therefore in *the shadow of Your wings* I will rejoice" (Ps. 63:7).

These verses may conjure up images of a mother hen with her chicks, but I promise you, the meaning is so much deeper than that!

The "shadow of God's wings" may seem an unusual metaphor to our Western ears, but this idiom makes more sense when you look closer at Jewish traditions and language. The Jewish prayer shawl, or *tallit*, is the modern equivalent of special garments worn by Jews since ancient times, but here's where things get extra interesting: The Hebrew word used for the tallit's "corners" is *kanafayim*, a word that may also be translated as "wings."[2] Thus, in the ancient world, Jews would have recognized that "the shadow of the Lord's wings" was a place of refuge and blessing because of its nearness to God. In modern times, the phrase, "'under the shadow of your wings' is a Hebraism meaning 'before YHVH in the place and state of worship.'"[3] In other words, Jews use this phrase to indicate intimacy with and adoration of God.

Now, reread the previous scriptures about the shadow of the Lord's wings. I hope you see that when you are walking through the valley of the shadow of death, praise gives you direct and privileged access to the "shadow of His wings"—the presence of your Heavenly Father where His lovingkindness is plentiful, where He keeps you safe from calamity, and where there is "fullness of joy."[4] Begin to praise Him in any way you are able, leaving behind the murky shades of grief to find shelter and blessing in the shadow of your Heavenly Father's wings.[5]

God Inhabits Our Praise

God is omnipotent (all-powerful), omniscient (all-knowing), and omnipresent (exists everywhere at every time), so since He lacks nothing, you may be wondering why He needs our praise at all. Well, on the one hand, He doesn't. Our praise or lack thereof does not change the facts of His power, knowledge, or existence. Praise does, however, affect our level of intimacy with the Lord in marvelous and unique ways, and closeness with us is His heart's desire. Moses and David had especially tight bonds with God, and they also recognized the relationship dynamics between the Lord and praise, so it makes sense to figure out what they knew about praise so that you can incorporate this into your grieving process as well.

When you think of a person from the Old Testament who would make a good worship leader, Moses probably doesn't immediately spring to mind, but just after the Red Sea crossing, Moses leads the Israelites in a lengthy song of praise. As he celebrates God's strength and thanks Him for their deliverance from the Egyptians, Moses proclaims, "The Lord is my strength and song, and He has become my salvation; He is my God, and I will praise Him."[6] The King James translation of the last part of this verse reads, "He is my God, and I will prepare him an habitation." *Nâvâh* is the Hebrew word translated as "praise" in the first translation and as "habitation" in the second, and it means "to rest as at home, to celebrate with praises; prepare an habitation."[7] In other words, our praise is both a celebration of our God and a dwelling place for Him.

About three hundred years later, David reinforces that last point in one of his most famous songs. In Psalm 22:3, David declares: "But thou art holy, O thou that inhabitest the praises [*tehillâh*] of Israel."[8] Some Bible translations read that God is "*enthroned* on/in the praises, of Israel" (emphasis added).[9] David's wording in this psalm implies that praise creates a royal dwelling place for the Lord much like a throne room for a king. Isn't this a remarkable thought? The book of Revelation speaks of God as the King sitting on His heavenly throne,[10] but have you ever considered the notion that our Father also makes His throne within the praises of His children?

I want to make one final connection between the type of praise David uses in this verse and Moses's use of the same word prior to the Children of Israel's crossing into the Promised Land. Moses reminds the people to fear the Lord, serve Him, love Him with all their heart, and praise Him: "He is your praise [tehillâh], and He is your God, who has done for you these great and awesome things which your eyes have seen."[11] Reread that verse and notice the significance of Moses's emphasis. He tells God's people to love and serve the Lord because *He* is their song of praise. Our Lord does not simply *evoke* praise. He is the recipient of praise, He lives in praise, and He is the substance of praise.

Think about what this means to the Church—and to you personally—to know God resides in and is the primary ingredient of your praise. Lifting your voice in praise during the most difficult of circumstances to provide a throne for the Lord could mean restoration and revival as it did for Ezra and the Israelites after the rebuilding of the temple in Jerusalem: "Stand up and bless [*bârak*] the Lord your God forever and ever! Blessed [bârak] be Your glorious name, which is exalted above all blessing and praise [tehillâh]!"[12] It could mean healing and salvation as it did for Jeremiah: "Heal me, O LORD, and I shall be healed; save me, and I shall be saved: for thou art my praise [tehillâh]."[13] It could also prompt a change in perspective as it did for the prophet Habakkuk and King David when they chose to praise the Lord while in the midst of lamentation.

Habakkuk's Perspective: Changed by Praise

Habakkuk was a prophet to Judah in the seventh century, BC, who spent much time in prayer, grieving over the sin and injustice he witnessed in God's Chosen People.[14] Therefore, Habakkuk's behavior after the Lord's revelation of Israel's impending invasion by the Chaldeans is nothing short of remarkable.[15] Yes, Habakkuk vents his feelings and complains to the Lord (steps 1 and 2 of lamentation), but then he determines to shut up, stand up, and set himself in a position to receive God's answer: "I will stand my watch and set myself on the rampart, and watch to see what He will say to me, and what I will answer when I am corrected."[16]

Did you catch that last part? Habakkuk expects God to answer him, but he also expects God to correct his faulty perceptions of the situation. Habakkuk is upset, disappointed, and scared, but instead of blaming or barking at God, he takes a position of humility and waits upon the Lord for insight.

When God answers Habakkuk, it's probably not at all what the prophet was hoping for, but his response is significant. Habakkuk deals with the news that worse times are on the horizon by (drum roll, please) remembering and recounting the Lord's goodness, majesty, faithfulness, and miraculous acts performed on behalf of His people. Habakkuk then acknowledges that he has heard God's words, and his subsequent praise reveals his understanding of who God is: "His glory covered the heavens, and the earth was full of His praise [tehillâh]."[17]

Habakkuk's act of remembrance and his recognition of God's authority beautifully transform his mindset. He transitions from a demonstration of fear of the future to expressions of praise and worship of the God who will preserve and strengthen him through his trials. This shift is located by the volta, "yet":

Though the fig tree may not blossom,
Nor fruit be on the vines;
Though the labor of the olive may fail,
And the fields yield no food;
Though the flock may be cut off from the fold,
And there be no herd in the stalls—
Yet I will rejoice in the Lord,
I will joy in the God of my salvation.
The Lord God is my strength;
He will make my feet like deer's feet,
And He will make me walk on my high hills.[18]

In other words, although the world may completely fall apart, Habakkuk declares he will still praise the Lord. I am convinced that Habakkuk's remembrance of and trust in the Lord are what enable him to ultimately praise God despite receiving answers to his prayers that defied expectations.

Oh, that we would all be like this prophet, recognizing that God knows better than we do and trusting that He will answer our prayers and clear up our murky understanding of difficult situations when we wait upon Him!

David's Perspective: Guided by Praise

Let's direct our attention now to another of David's lamentations to see how his perspective is guided by the various forms of praise he uses in Psalm 34. David wrote this psalm in Gath (a city in the territory of Israel's great enemy, the Philistines) after dodging King Saul's numerous attempts to kill him. Achish, the king of Gath, recognizes David as the guy who has slain thousands of Philistines, so to avoid getting killed, David pretends to be crazy, and the king kicks him out of the city. David is hiding in the caves of Adullam when he writes the following words:[19]

I will bless [bârak] the Lord at all times;

His praise [tehillâh] shall continually be in my mouth.

My soul shall make its boast [hâlal] in the Lord;

The humble shall hear of it and be glad.

Oh, magnify the Lord with me,

And let us exalt his name together.

I sought the Lord, and he heard me,

And delivered me from all my fears.[20]

It is amazing that after nearly being murdered by the king of Israel and narrowly escaping from the king of an enemy nation, David has the where-withal to kneel before the Lord in adoration, to sing a song of praise that exalts the name of the Lord, and to say he will do so "at all times"—even the cruddy times!

God Is Good **All** *the* **Time**

David's use of past tense in verses four and six of Psalm 34 is also significant because this indicates his assurance of God's abilities. The man is still hiding in a cave as he writes this song, yet he twice professes that the Lord has heard his cries and has already delivered him from the things that are creating fear within him![21] David goes on to explain that he's not a special case; God also hears the cries of all His children, and He is more than capable and willing to help them when they need it.[22]

David's praise also shows that he doesn't allow his circumstances to skew his perception of God's character. Yes, bad things have happened, and the difficult times are not over yet, but David isn't waiting for his circumstances to change before he believes that the Lord has heard him and paved the way to safety. While still in the midst of turmoil, David acknowledges that God is trustworthy and therefore worthy of praise: "Oh, taste and see that the Lord is good; blessed is the man who trusts in Him!...But those who seek the Lord shall not lack any good thing."[23]

David recognizes that God is good *all the time*. In fact, several of David's psalms were written at dangerous or devastating times in his life, and in all of these, David never fails to magnify the Lord.[24] In each of these psalms, it is evident that David recognizes that his current situation does not negate the goodness or majesty of his God.

Sister, no matter what your eyes see, what your heart feels, or what other people might say, remember this: God is in His heaven, He is in control, and He is ever faithful and always good.

God Is Near to the Brokenhearted

I cannot leave the discussion of this psalm without addressing the verse that has encouraged me and so many others during moments of heartbreak. In Psalm 34:18, David assures us of the nearness our Heavenly Father at such times: "The Lord is close to the brokenhearted and saves those who are crushed in spirit."[25] Although your loss may make it seem as if God is a million miles away, please know, sister, He is oh, so near. Your Heavenly Father longs for you to reach out your arms to Him when you are hurting. David's lament is a reminder that if you would but call out to the Lord, He will hear you; He will come to you; and He will gather you in His arms, tuck you into the secret place of His presence, and minister peace and life to you.

Impacts of Praise on the Enemy

There is a bit of science behind the effects of praise: For every action praise performs upon us, there is an equal and opposite effect upon our enemy. Praise liberates us and binds the enemy. Praise advances our progress and stops the enemy's. Praise strengthens us and weakens the enemy. Praise opens our eyes to the truth and muffles our enemy's voice.[26] All of this is possible because praise breaks our fixation on the enemy's tactics and redirects our attention to the Lord. How our enemy must hate it when we praise the Lord because praise thwarts his plans and gives us victory!

The primary effect of praise on Satan is he can't operate through us when we are praising the Lord. Anger, unforgiveness, distraction, worry—any and all weapons in his arsenal are dulled, if not destroyed, when our focus is directed upon the Lord and not our circumstances. For example, it is impossible to worry when we are communing with the Almighty God, King of heaven and earth. When we praise Him, the Lord breaks the chains the enemy uses to bind us, much as He did for Paul and Silas in their jail cell.

Just a few days before He would be crucified, Jesus also reveals that praise gives us strength to fight against the enemy. In response to the priests' complaints that children are praising Jesus outside the temple, the Lord responds, "Out of the mouth of babes and nursing infants You have perfected praise."[27] Christ's quoting of Psalm 8:2 exposes an additional layer of meaning to this verse, emphasizing that humble, childlike praise of the Lord will "silence the enemy and the avenger."[28]

So when the devil comes to you in those midnight hours, wreaking havoc on your emotions and whispering lies into your ear that God is far away or unconcerned about your loss, go on the offensive. Praising the Lord and thanking Him for His promises puts a gag order on your enemy and ushers in the peace that passes understanding—the peace of God's Truth!

God's Faithfulness in My Grief

The Lord ultimately blessed my husband and me with two more children after our miscarriages. Several months after the "volta" turning point in my grief process (when I made the decision to remember the goodness of my God), and after four years of trying to get pregnant, I conceived my son, Mitchell. I called him my little "balm of Gilead" because his birth symbolized hope and restoration to me.[29] Our final child, Patrick, was an unexpected but delightful bonus blessing who came twenty-two months later

Throughout my pregnancy with Mitchell, I often sang Thomas O. Chisholm's "Great Is Thy Faithfulness," a hymn inspired by three verses from a poem of lamentation written by the prophet Jeremiah (see Appendix I).[30]

Singing this song brought unspeakable peace to my heart and was my way of thanking the Lord for His great faithfulness to me and my family. I selected this song to be played at Mitchell's dedication service when he was three months old as a declaration that the Lord is indeed faithful no matter what we may be going through.

Dwell on these words by Jeremiah. Despite his despair over Jerusalem's destruction, Jeremiah made a conscious decision to focus upon the mercy, compassion, and faithfulness of the Lord:

> This I recall to mind,
> Therefore I have hope:
> Through the Lord's mercies we are not consumed,
> Because His compassions fail not.
> They are new every morning;
> Great is your faithfulness.[31]

These verses from the book of Lamentations encapsulate the healing process that began in me over two decades ago and continues to this day. I chose then, and I choose now to remember my Lord's faithfulness to me in times past. I acknowledged then and now that although I have undergone trauma, the Lord has preserved me. I recognized then and now that God's compassion is renewed and available for me to receive each and every day because of His loving mercy.

When things don't make sense, when I don't understand, when I am weak and weary from crying, I will remember the Lord and who He is. My eyes cannot see everything, but His do. My wisdom is incomplete, but His is all-encompassing. I will choose to hope and trust in the Lord, for He can and will change my mourning into gladness by laying upon my shoulders the garment of praise and by taking me into the shelter of His wings.

Jesus began and ended His earthly ministry by quoting and directing our attention to Isaiah 61 and Psalm 22, poems that not only emphasize the Lord's sovereignty and divinity but also detail the lamentation process.[32] Remember, Jesus promised difficulties would come our way; however, isn't it marvelous to consider how the Lord, during events in His earthly ministry that were fraught with stress and turmoil, guided us to scriptures that contain the patterns of lamentation? We can take comfort in a God who provides and demonstrates a process of mourning that acts as both rudder and telescope, helping us navigate tribulations and the turbulent seas of grief. [33]

As we complete this section on the lamentation process, I pray you come to intimately understand the effectiveness of God's pattern for mourning. Lamentation directs our prayer life, allowing us to give voice to our innermost thoughts and feelings, and it keeps our focus on God, ensuring that we do not lose sight of Him or our faith in Him. Grief ebbs and flows, and when you feel a wave trying to take you under, dive into lamentation.

Apply CCRRE or a mnemonic device of your own that helps you to remember the lamentation process, and put it into practice (see Appendix J for a sample guide). When you go to the Lord with your sorrow over your precious little one, He will escort you through the billows of grief to dry land. As you cry out and complain to the Lord, request of and remember Him, and express your praise to Him, your relationship with your Heavenly Father will deepen, and intimacy with the Lord is what brings restoration after loss.

After loss...it is a bit of an understatement to say life is different after your baby passes, and sometimes it may feel as though you are merely going through the motions or walking in a fog. In Part 3 of this book, I provide practical tips for navigating life and relationships after loss. So take a deep breath, take the hand of your Heavenly Father, and take a bold step toward hope and peace.

1. Strong, *Strong's Exhaustive Concordance*, under "H6738: "*tsêl*: shadow, shade."

2. McLelland, *Jesus and Women*, 19. Num. 15:37–40; Juhasz, "tzitzit," in *Encyclopedia of Jewish Folklore and Traditions*; Wigoder et al., eds. "Tallit," in *The New Encyclopedia of Judaism*. The tallit is a reminder of the Lord's commandments, symbolizes His names, and is worn for prayer services and when blessings are read from the Torah.

3. Lawrence, "Abiding Under the Shadow of His Wings."

4. Ps. 16:11.

5. Look to the Bible as well as Chapter 8 and Appendices G and H for inspiration.

6. Exod. 15:2.

7. Strong, *Strong's Exhaustive Concordance*, under "H5115, *nâvâh*."

8. KJV. Strong, *Strong's Exhaustive Concordance*, under "H8416, *tehillâh*: song of praise, adoration, glory."

9. AMP, CSB, ESV, NIV, NKJV, NLT, and NASB.

10. Rev. 4:2.

11. Deut. 10:21.

12. Neh. 9:5. Strong, *Strong's Exhaustive Concordance*, under "H1288, *bârak*: to kneel; to bless God."

13. Jer. 17:14.

14. Habakkuk lived at the same time as Zephaniah, Jeremiah, and Ezekial, prophets who shared the same distress over the condition of the children of Israel.

15. Hab. 1:5–6. This invasion occurs because the Israelites have continued in their sin against God despite His repeated warnings.

16. Hab. 1:13–2:1.

17. Hab. 3:3.

18. Hab. 3:17–19.

19. 1 Sam. 21:13–15; 1 Sam. 22:1–3.

20. Ps. 34:1–4.

21. Ps. 34:4, 6.

22. Ps. 34:15, 17.

23. Ps. 34:8, 10.

24. David's son, Absolom, was trying to steal David's throne (Ps. 3). Cush was lying to Saul about David, telling him David was trying to kill Saul (Ps. 7). David's sin with Bathsheba was exposed by Nathan the prophet (Ps. 51). Mourning Saul's slaughter of eighty-five people, including Ahimelech, priests, and their wives and children (Ps. 52). Betrayal by the Ziphites and escaping death by Saul's hand (Psalm 54). More songs written in the caves of Adullam as he hid from Saul (Pss. 56 and 142). David spares Saul's life in a cave (Ps. 57). King Saul tried to kill David in his own home (Ps. 59). Again fleeing from Saul into the wilderness of Judea (Ps. 63).

25. NIV

26. 2 Chron. 20:22; Ps. 8:2; Ps. 188:14; Ps. 149:6; Is. 12:22; Acts 16:25; James 4:7.

27. Matt. 21:16.

28. Wommack, *The Effects of Praise*.

29. Jer. 8:22.

30. Gabriel, *The Singers and Their Songs*. The prophet Jeremiah's words inspired Chisholm to pen "Great is Thy Faithfulness" as he reflected upon the faithfulness of His Heavenly Father during the unexpected twists and turns of his own life. The poem was ultimately set to music by William M. Runyan. Chisholm is the author of over 1,200 poems.

31. Lam. 3:21–23.

32. In Luke 4:16–21, Jesus reads Isaiah 61:1–2 in the synagogue, declaring, "Today, this Scripture is fulfilled in your hearing." During His crucifixion, Jesus quotes Psalm 22:1 when He cries, "My God, My God, why have you forsaken me?" (Matt. 27:46; Mark 15:34).

33. John 16:33.

Part 3:

LIFE AFTER LOSS

MERRY HEART MINISTRIES

Weep with Those Who Weep

When Jesus saw her weeping,
and the Jews who came with her weeping,
He groaned in the spirit and was troubled....
Jesus wept.
JOHN 11:33, 35

WAVES OF GRIEF TEND to arrive unannounced, and after each of my miscarriages, tears fell unexpectedly, involuntarily, and frequently. I had a wonderful network of loved ones who volunteered their shoulders to cry upon, but as the months and sadness wore on, I became concerned about my lingering grief becoming a burden to family and friends. I therefore chose to weep in solitude before the Lord, and although I knew in my spirit that He was always with me, I still craved the consolation of human contact: a pair of arms to enfold me, ears to listen to me, and eyes to look into mine with kinship and understanding.

Our Heavenly Father made us this way, you know. We yearn for the love and support of others because companionship has been a part of God's design for human life from the very beginning. After creating Adam, our Heavenly Father pronounced, "It is not good that man should be alone," so He crafted Eve, a mate suited to Adam in every way.[1] In his wisdom, Solomon declared, "Two are better than one" because he recognized the human need for assistance, especially when we fall.[2] The apostle Paul (not known for his brevity) took only one sentence to express the importance of being there for others in the highs and the lows of life: "Rejoice with those who rejoice, and *weep with those who weep*" (emphasis added).[3]

Although these scriptures reveal the necessity of supporting one another in work, play, and celebration, there appears to be an emphasis on sustaining one another *in sorrow*. We humans need companionship to provide physical, emotional, and spiritual aid when our bodies are weak, our nerves are shot, and our shields of faith are embedded with the enemy's arrows. It's been said that misery loves company; I would counter that misery is *eased* by company, for the weight of grief is truly easier to bear when the burden is shared, and weeping with others who have also shed the tears of loss facilitates healing in ways you may not fully comprehend.

The Solace of Shared Experiences

There was a component of my mourning that many could not touch because, simply put, they hadn't "walked in my shoes." Prior to my first miscarriage, infant loss was rarely mentioned among relatives and friends, and since I knew few people who had had a miscarriage, one of the hardest parts of my grieving process was the inability to discuss or explain my struggles with someone who could relate to my pain.

A few days after my first miscarriage, I received a visit from one of my aunts. Twenty-five years before, she had lost her six-month-old son to SIDS, and as she entered my living room, the empathy in her eyes didn't need verbal expression. She held me to her heart with a knowing embrace that communicated a deep and personal awareness of what it meant to lose a baby. My aunt's willingness to share my pain immediately lifted the weight from my shoulders in a way that surprised me and imparted a rare gift of comfort and peace.

There is something very freeing about being with others who have been through a similar experience of infant loss. You don't have to try to frame your words into something the other person can comprehend. They just *know*. They understand how your body feels, how your heart is aching, and what life in the future will look like. One of the mothers I interviewed described it this way: "Those who walked through miscarriage knew exactly what to say." Mamas whose hearts have been broken know better than most what will soothe yours.

Therefore, if no one in your circle has experienced miscarriage or infant loss, consider joining a support group. Check with your doctor or pastor about the availability of infant-loss support systems, and/or browse the internet for information on support groups in your area.[4] Spend time with other parents who have suffered loss—they are often able to provide guidance through difficult moments and to share coping skills that have worked for them.

Talking Through the Tears

Oftentimes, the support you need most from others is the freedom to speak about your baby and your loss. One study on perinatal mourning found that for many grieving parents, "sharing stories about the deceased with others" was deemed more helpful than talking things out with a professional.[5] In fact, some of the mothers I interviewed noted that they received greater comfort from talking about their baby than from *any other* form of sympathy. One mother suggested that conversations about Baby are beneficial to both the speaker and the listener: "Tell your full story to someone. It needs to be heard."

Yet another mother whose son lived just a few minutes after birth explained the importance of being able to speak about her son's short life with others:

> I would like others to know that it is okay to ask about our baby
> and loss. Pretending like it didn't happen is much more painful,

and in fact, I enjoy talking about our baby—it keeps his memory alive. People sometimes think that by bringing up our loss, they are reminding us that he died, but that is not true. They are not reminding me, because I have not forgotten for a single minute. I am acutely aware of the loss on a daily basis.

Your own acute awareness of your loss should be expressed to others as well. Let people know that it is healing for you to be allowed to have conversations about your little one.

Unfortunately, some of the parents I interviewed felt an inability to talk about their babies' passing or to express their pain because family and friends stopped asking about it. One mother told me that after early inquiries about her loss, "it was never discussed or brought up [again]." Another mother lamented, "I feel like everybody just said, 'Sorry,' and that was it. No follow ups. No checking in. No seeing how I was doing initially or later. It was almost like a very taboo thing [to talk about it]." This failure (or refusal) to mention Baby was perceived by some of the parents I interviewed as an indication that others lacked interest, were uncomfortable with infant loss, or thought the parents talked about it too much. As a result, grieving parents no longer felt at liberty to mention their babies around others and kept their pain inside.

Scientists call this inability to express sorrow "silenced grief" which, whether others realize it or not, denies parents their right to grieve and makes parents feel they've been pushed to the margins.[6] Unfortunately, when grief is silenced like this, depression is more likely to occur, and parents progress through their mourning process much more slowly.[7]

Dear sister, if you have not been allowed to express your grief, it is imperative that you find a way to do so. If family or friends are not comfortable with being your sounding board, find a support group or person who will enable you to talk through your sorrow. Although it's valuable to speak with others who have also endured grief, know that sympathetic hearts don't beat solely within the chests of those who have endured trials similar to yours. The work of the Holy Spirit is able to be accomplished through caring, compassionate souls who are willing to support you in your mourning process, so when you find one of these kindred spirits, lean into this precious gift of the Lord.

Weeping with Your Spouse

Although family members, friends, and support groups make useful and effective counselors and comforters, you must also make a point of grieving with your spouse. This may seem intuitive and obvious advice, but death has a way of clouding our thoughts or blinding us to what the Lord intends for marriage. You and your spouse are two parts of a whole, and when one of you is suffering, you both suffer. As spouses, your primary duties are to encourage, support, and pray for one another, and these things are easier to accomplish when you carve out time to lament together and are honest about your needs and your feelings.

However, it's important to keep in mind that your patterns for grief may not always be in alignment. My husband mourned our babies' losses, but he didn't feel the same sense of sudden isolation and emptiness that I did, so our approaches to grieving were naturally asymmetrical. This situation is not unique to my hubby and me, so it is essential to recognize that you and your baby's father are two different people with different ways of experiencing and expressing sorrow. In fact, a perinatal grief study by Lang et al. found that the ways men and women deal with grief are often at odds with one another:

> Within couples, spouses had different expectations about how to react, how to behave and what was an appropriate length of time to grieve....[W]omen needed to talk about the loss for a longer time than men. Couples reported that these divergent expectations created marital tension and limited the amount of support they could offer each other.[8]

It's not just that you are two different people — it's that you're two different *grieving* people, and the dissimilarities in the ways men and women deal with grief are often striking. Don't be surprised or annoyed if you and the baby's father seem to be on separate grief cycles (or even separate planets).

Men tend to process perinatal loss in a much quieter, less demonstrative, unobtrusive way. In fact, one hundred percent of the mothers I interviewed stated that the fathers' methods for dealing with miscarriages and stillbirths were unlike theirs. The men shed fewer tears, talked about the experience less, and visibly grieved for a shorter period of time. Only one father was able to initially express his feelings as openly as his wife who stated he was "very present" during the early days of grieving. Another mother explained that her husband displayed little emotion with their first miscarriage but became "more emotional and vulnerable" with each of the next two miscarriages. Forty percent of the mothers used the words "sad" to describe the fathers' grief, but only 47% mentioned that their husbands cried or were "emotional" in their presence, and this emotion was typically expressed only on the day the loss occurred. Two mothers noted that their husbands took charge of the family and household duties or busied themselves with projects as a "distraction" for their grief.

The reasons for fathers' relative inexpressiveness are varied. Some men feel left out when medical personnel, friends, and family focus mainly (or solely) on the needs of the baby's mother. Others avoid displays of emotion to prevent further distressing their wives. Twenty percent of the women I interviewed specifically mentioned their husbands' protective natures as a reason for their stoicism. The only father who volunteered to be interviewed for this book stated that he consciously stifled his grief in his wife's presence because he wished to protect her feelings. However, he also noted that his failure to mourn negatively affected him long afterward:

> I did not grieve at the time; I stuffed it down inside. My role was to be supportive of my wife. Years later when I had the loss of the marriage, all my grief started to come out and I was not able to control it. I went to therapy and a group called Compassionate Friends (support group for those who had lost a child).

Unfortunately, just as with women, there are typically negative consequences for fathers who fail to process their grief, so encourage your baby's father to find outlets for his sorrow and to seek additional support when he needs it.

Both parents must also recognize that it is essential for them to find ways to process their grief if they want to maintain a healthy marriage. One mother I interviewed noted the adverse effects of her husband's inability to understand her grieving process: "My husband was extremely distant and didn't really understand why I was so depressed. It took a toll on our marriage." Research has shown that "women who experienced miscarriage and stillbirth had significantly greater odds of divorce than women without a loss," and couples enduring stillbirth have even greater odds of divorce than those whose babies are lost to miscarriage.[9] Unfortunately, 13.3% of the parents whom I interviewed divorced as a direct result of perinatal loss, with one mother explaining that her marriage ended because she lost respect for her husband after her miscarriage.

The loss of a child is one of the hardest things you will have to navigate within your marriage, and extending the same degree of grace and patience that you would wish to receive will go a long way in increasing marriage stability. Because each parent's needs are rarely on the same page at any given moment, it is crucial that you spend time in prayer (together and separately), asking the Lord for peace, strength, and the ability to recognize and meet the other's needs.

Weeping with the Lord

As you discovered through the process of lamentation, your Heavenly Father desires for you to come to Him in your pain and to "cast your cares upon Him"; however, what you may not always remember is that He grieves over your sorrow. When you cry out to Him in your sorrow, and when you weep in His presence, He cries too.[10]

Let us first look to the way in which the Lord dealt with the death of John the Baptist to illustrate this point. Scripture tells us that after He was told about Herod's beheading of John the Baptist, Jesus "departed from there by boat to a deserted place by Himself."[11] Jesus leaves the crowds that have been following

Him to process His loss and the grief that accompanied it, and His way of processing is to hurry away to mourn with His Heavenly Father. Jesus knows that strength and peace are found in His Father's presence, and I am confident that Jesus wept over John's death.

I have this confidence because of Jesus's response to the death of His good friend, Lazarus. The Lord knew Lazarus had died before He departed for Bethany, so Jesus would not have been surprised to see Lazarus's sister, Mary, crying upon His arrival, but the Bible says, "When Jesus saw her weeping, and the Jews who came with her weeping, He *groaned in the spirit and was troubled*" (emphasis added).[12] After He is told where the body of Lazarus is laid, the Bible emphasizes that "Jesus wept," and on His way to the tomb, Jesus is "again groaning in Himself."[13] What stands out to me about this event is Jesus's emotional state despite knowing what is about to happen: He is literally on His way to resurrect Lazarus from the dead, yet Jesus still *grieves*. He still experiences deep sorrow when witnessing the grief of others and suffers disappointment and anguish over the death of His friend. The story of Lazarus's death and resurrection reveals to us a Savior who weeps with those who weep because He is genuinely overcome with the emotions (His own as well as those of others) associated with loss.

Jesus told His disciples, "He who has seen Me has seen the Father," so if Jesus cried over the loss of life and the heartache of others, we can be assured that our Heavenly Father does as well.[14] Let this sink in a moment because this also applies to your loss. I love how King David expresses this idea: "You keep track of all my sorrows. / You have collected all my tears in your bottle. / You have recorded each one in your book."[15]

Weep with your Heavenly Father, dear sister. Recognize that He finds the life of your baby precious, and He finds the death of your baby precious. He grieves the fact that you are in pain, and He cries along with you.

Just as others have mingled their tears with yours, sadly and inevitably, you will have the opportunity to do the same with another parent experiencing similar pain. You see, "weeping with those who weep" has double meaning: It is an action that imparts blessing to you in your sorrow, and it is a method of blessing others in their sorrow as well.

---

1. Gen. 2:18.

2. Eccl. 4:9–12.

3. Rom. 12:15.

4. Here are a few miscarriage and infant-loss grief resources. **Christian miscarriage support**: https://christianliferesources.com/what-we-do/services/pregnancy-and-infant-loss. **Idaho miscarriage support resources**: https://www.miscarriageresources.com/idaho-miscarriage-resources. **Empty Cradle: Pregnancy and Infant Loss Support, Remembrance and Education**: https://www.emptycradle.org/

5. Mitima-Verloop et al., "Facilitating Grief," 742.

6. Figueredo-Borda et al., "Experiences of Miscarriage, 782; Cassidy, "The Disenfranchisement."

7. Cassidy, "The Disenfranchisement"; Figueredo-Borda et al., "Experiences of Miscarriage."

8. Lang et al., "Perinatal Loss," 190.

9. Shreffler et al., "Exploring the Increased Odds of Divorce," 104.

10. 1 Pet. 5:7.

11. Mt. 14:13; cf. Mk. 6:32; Lk. 9:10.

12. John 11:14, 33.

13. Jn. 11:35, 38. *Strong's Exhaustive Concordance*, under "G1690, embrimaomai.";
Collins Dictionary, under "chagrin: a feeling of vexation, marked by disappointment
or humiliation." https://www.collinsdictionary.com/dictionary/english/chagrin. To
help you better identify and understand the deep emotions Jesus displayed here,
we need to examine the original language. The Greek word for "groaned" in these
passages is *embrimaomai* which means "to snort with anger; to have indignation;
to sigh with chagrin." The latter definition seems the logical option for what is
happening at Lazarus's tomb since chagrin is defined as "a feeling of vexation, marked
by disappointment or humiliation."

14. John 14:9.

15. Ps. 56:8, NLT.

CHAPTER ELEVEN

Turning Your Trials into Trails

Gracious words are a honeycomb,
Sweet to the soul and healing to the bones.
PROVERBS 16:24, NIV

WHEN WE CHRISTIANS HAVE "been there and done that," when we have crossed through the darkness of the valley of mourning and made it back into the light, we have, whether we realize it or not, blazed a trail. What a shame to hide that trail under the veil of secrecy so that others miss the benefit of following in our footsteps. If we have the map to get through rough terrain and the ability to gently guide others to firmer footing, we need to do so!

One of the mothers I interviewed explained how she was able to bless other grieving mothers with insights she'd gained from navigating infant loss herself: "Many friends have opened up to me about their own experiences with child-loss, and I felt that I had a new perspective to be able to sympathize with them and understand." Sharing our experiences of infant loss with one another enables us to provide comfort to those who might otherwise be left to tend their wounded hearts themselves. Offering empathetic comfort to others is also what the apostle Paul encouraged the early Church to do:

> Blessed be the God and Father of our Lord Jesus Christ, the Father of mercies and God of all comfort, who comforts us in all our tribulation, that we may be able to comfort those who are in any trouble, with the comfort with which we ourselves are comforted by God.[1]

Thus, just as the Lord supports and aids us in our grief, we should come alongside others in theirs.

Ninety-three percent of the parents I interviewed expressed the need for acknowledgement of and support for their loss, so the purpose of this chapter is to illustrate methods of providing support for those who are grieving. Included here are parents' responses to interview questions that dealt with the types of condolences they received—the good, the bad, and the ugly. I share these responses for two primary reasons: 1) Every parent grieving the loss of a little one needs to hear that they are not alone on this journey; and 2) These responses serve as a reference for offering more effective consolation to others.

The Power of Silent Presence

The need for companionship during times of loss often trumps the need for words of comfort. Some people may find this surprising because we humans like to "fix" things, and because we know there is nothing we can do about the loss itself, we often feel the need to fill the void in the mourner's life with words—our own or those of the Lord's.

Two of the mothers I interviewed emphasized that words of counsel are often not what grieving parents need or want to hear, especially in the early days after loss. One of these mothers explained it this way: "Sometimes we don't want to get advice from people. Sometimes we just want to feel loved, seen, and heard." Another mother expressed the importance of simply being there for parents in mourning:

> I would hesitate to give advice to a grieving mother. I would only want to love on them with the love of Jesus, ask them about their baby, remember with them, and give them a place to remember and talk about their baby. I guess I would want to encourage them to embrace their child's memory and cherish it.

In essence, more than recommendations or guidance, grieving parents want companionship and love.

As a matter of fact, silent presence often creates solidarity in times of extreme sorrow. Contrary to what some may think, "silence is not a rejection or dismissal" of someone's pain.[2] It is instead an acknowledgement that one cannot truly know what another grieving person is going through. One of the mothers I interviewed provided this advice for grieving parents:

> Find a support system of family and friends that will sit with you in your pain without rushing you to move on or feeling like they have to say the perfect thing to make you feel better—ones that will sit in silence with you, or go on walks to talk about it, or go on walks without talking about it at all.

You see, far from being a sign of disrespect, silence is often a caring way of reverencing the other's loss while simultaneously supplying support and strength.

This very idea is emphasized in the biblical story of Job. This poor man experienced extreme and unimaginable hardship: the deaths of multiple sons and daughters in addition to the loss of his livestock, property, wealth, and health. Upon hearing of Job's tribulations, three of his friends came to him, "sat down with him on the ground seven days and seven nights, and no one spoke a word to him, for they saw that his grief was very great."[3]

Job's friends joined him in his grief—they met him where he was, on the ground and in the depths of despair—and because they recognized the magnitude of his grief, *they said nothing*. They knew during those seven days that there were no words in human language that could be expressed to relieve his pain, so they remained silent. Their presence and willingness to grieve with him was the very support Job required in those moments.

When Words to Comfort Others Are Hard to Find

Many people find it difficult to talk about miscarriage, infant loss, and stillbirth because these losses are not only tragic, but they are also frequently accompanied by suffering, mystery, and misunderstanding. You will likely notice that some of those who attempt to console you are going to be uncomfortable and probably won't know what to say. Parents whom I interviewed for this book stated that others' uneasiness often translated into their failure to even acknowledge that there was a loss. One mother I interviewed noted the pain caused when family members ignored her miscarriage:

> My family was wonderful and very respectful of our loss. My husband's family not so much [*sic*]. We told them of the miscarriage, [but] it was seen as not a big deal. They still do not acknowledge [the baby's] life. This had a huge impact on me.

In contrast, two other parents pointed out that it eased the tension when people were honest about their loss for words. One mother in particular told me about a conversation with a friend who came by her house after she had lost her son at twenty-eight weeks:

> Our neighbor came over and just acted normal with us. It was so
> nice. Everyone up to that point was acting so strange around us.
> When he came over, he said, "I don't know what to say or do, so
> I will just be myself." [My husband and I] started to laugh and
> cry at the same time. It freaked [our neighbor] out. We were like,
> "No, thank you for being normal." That [was] what we needed.

The truth of the matter is there isn't much that people can say to make a grieving person feel better, so sincerity is a good place to start. If you are in mourning, be honest with others about your needs. If you are offering consolation to others, tell them that you don't know what to say and ask how best to support them.

Don't underestimate the power of human contact either; this often speaks louder than words. Sometimes, the comfort I needed most was found in my own mother's presence, feeling the touch of her hand or the warmth of her embrace. One parent in my study explained that a hug from a woman who had previously experienced a miscarriage brought her great comfort "because she understood that there are not proper words to say. She understood that the grief and experience, while shared, [are] still deeply personal." This hug, which resulted from a recognition of shared experience, was able to cut through the sorrow and minister empathy and compassion to a mama's broken heart more than her words possibly could.

When Words of Comfort Are Not Very Comforting

I received some wonderful condolence cards, flowers, and phone calls from various family members and friends after both miscarriages; however, there were unexpected difficulties with some of the verbal condolences I received. Most people were sympathetic to my feelings, and the majority of their sentiments were consoling. Some said, "I'm praying for you," or "I'm so sorry for your loss," but every now and then, a person said something like, "Well, at least you already have two children" or "This was probably for the best because there must have been something wrong with the baby." Although I knew that their words were well intended and that no one meant to cause me pain, comments such as these were like needles piercing my heart.

I mention this because 87% of the parents I surveyed stated that they received less-than-comforting condolences after infant loss.[4] This discovery was tremendously eye-opening because I truly did not expect negative commentary to be this pervasive or for there to be so many similarities in the types of condolences participants received. Then I remembered Job's friends again. They comforted Job in their silence, but things got complicated when they opened their mouths to give advice. After pondering this, I came to the following not-so-earth-shattering conclusion: People are imperfect, and if they don't seek guidance from the Lord, they may say something more hurtful than helpful.

Two mothers I interviewed spoke pointedly about painful "condolences." One advised, "Don't take what people say about your loss or grief to heart. People who haven't gone through it don't know what to say and they don't understand how you feel." The other mother provided this insight on the cause of hurtful words: "Some family members said silly things that were thoughtless. They wouldn't have said them if they had thought twice."

It should come as no surprise that in their effort to fill uncomfortable silences, people sometimes speak before considering the implications of their words. Therefore, to help readers "think twice" about their condolences, I want to briefly mention two categories of comments—logical and religious/philosophical—that were frequently noted by parents I interviewed as particularly upsetting.

Logic-Based "Condolences"

Attempts at approaching miscarriage with logic or practicality were viewed by parents as hurtful because such comments seemed to downplay the significance of their loss. One mother was told, "You can try again," and another was told that she was "still young." Although these statements were true, they brought no comfort to either mother. The first mother noted that the comment made her feel "as though [her] baby was not a unique human being who mattered—as though [she] could just go get another one and everything would be better." This mother's perspective is understandable because most parents who have experienced perinatal loss truly wish "to have their babies acknowledged as irreplaceable individuals."[5] Thus, for parents grieving miscarriage, recommendations for subsequent pregnancies often take an emotional toll on an already wounded heart.

Especially painful to parents were logic-based remarks which suggested that miscarriage was a common or natural occurrence. When people told one mother I interviewed that miscarriage "was normal," she said it made her feel "as if [she] shouldn't be sad because it was common and no big deal." The father who lost six babies to miscarriage described to me the effects of people's attempts to normalize this type of loss:

> With the first miscarriage, most people expressed condolences and then told a story of their miscarriage or of someone they knew who had miscarried. They told it as an expression of there being hope or that it happens to a lot of people. After multiple miscarriages, people really didn't say much. They had no way to identify or show a connecting experience. The less they said, the less we shared, and we were isolated.

Decades after his losses, the pain of this father's grief drips from the page. Yes, miscarriages happen to parents around the world every day, but frequency isn't equivalent to commonness. Each event brings its own special kind of pain.

Another unsuccessful form of condolence described by parents I spoke with was the use of the phrase "at least" to precede pretty much any sentence. Here are a few examples of such statements along with the grieving mothers' responses:

- "At least you know you can get pregnant."
  This was expressed to multiple parents, and one noted that although true, being told this after her loss was "not soothing in the moment." Another mother explained, "This was especially painful because I'd

experienced infertility problems before and after the miscarriage."

- "At least you weren't that far along."
  The mother who was told this said, "It almost makes you feel worse and invalid for the sadness you feel."

- "At least you have other children."
  This negated the feelings of sadness for the baby who was lost.

As one mother explained, "Any and all 'at least' statements are painful." To put it plainly, such statements are painful because they minimize the sorrow of grieving parents.

Although the intention behind "at least" statements may be good, this attempt at optimism is poorly timed because most people who are in the early stages of grief are not ready to be optimistic. It is unrealistic to expect grieving parents to "look on the bright side" of things while they are still groping in the darkness cast by death's shadow. In Proverbs, King Solomon described the effects of out-of-place optimism: "Singing cheerful songs to a person with a heavy heart is like taking someone's coat in cold weather or pouring vinegar in a wound."[6] The bottom line is that logic-based remarks aren't typically the kinds of lifelines people grasp when they feel they are drowning in grief.

This is probably one of the reasons why the apostle Paul tells us to weep with those who weep. Sometimes, gazing into the tear-filled eyes of another person when we are grieving creates an instant bond that is far more comforting than any attempt at positivity could be.

Religious or Philosophical "Condolences"

Now we come to the religious or philosophical types of condolences that parents I interviewed perceived as unhelpful or downright hurtful. Several mothers were told things like, "It wasn't meant to be," or "There is a reason for everything." Some Christian mothers heard variations of, "This was God's way of protecting you from a child with a handicap or illness," or "This was God's will." One mother's reaction to being told her miscarriage was a "part of God's plan" is a particularly heart-wrenching illustration of why such words should not be spoken to a grieving parent:

> While that might be true, that is hard to understand, and it is immensely frustrating to be told that God's plan involved taking [my] baby but letting other people keep theirs....It is incredibly frustrating and sometimes feels like we are being punished for something.

These last words tormented me for days after I read them. I ached for this mother and for every other parent who questioned after their loss, "Why *my* baby, Lord? What did I do wrong?"

Dear sister, permit me a bit of a detour because someone needs to know this: *Your baby's death was not a form of punishment.*

Baby's Death Was *Not* God's Punishment

When there are no reasons or explanations for our babies' losses, it is easy to blame ourselves or God for what happened, believing we must have done something wrong physically or spiritually. Let's nip that thinking in the bud right now; it's dangerous to go down that path because these mindsets tend to increase and lengthen grief.[7]

Two parents I interviewed specifically wished to encourage parents in mourning who may be struggling with feelings of shame or guilt. One stressed, "You did nothing wrong," and another mother wanted grieving parents to know, "There is nothing 'wrong' with them. They are not being 'punished' for anything they have done." You must understand that the belief that the Lord is punishing you is a lie of the enemy intended to keep you in sorrow and to separate you from the love of your Heavenly Father.

If anyone dare point to the Bible via the Second Commandment or to the death of King David and Bathsheba's infant as examples of God's punishing children for parental wrongdoing, counter these arguments with Mosaic law and the knowledge of God's unchanging character.

First of all, when the Second Commandment says that the Lord's punishment for those who make and worship carved images will also extend to "children to the third and fourth generations of those who hate Me," the Lord is speaking of the punishment for *idolatry*—rejection of God as the one and only God.[8] This is a sin that tends to be taught from one generation to the next, so the punishment for this sin would also follow from generation to generation.

The Bible explicitly states that the sins of fathers are, in fact, *not* laid on the children who are innocent of their parent's sin. The following examples outline this fact:

1. Moses decrees, "Fathers shall not be put to death for their children, nor shall children be put to death for their father; a person shall be put to death for his own sin."[9]

2. King Amaziah cites this same Mosaic law when he refuses to execute the children of the men who murdered his father, Joash.[10]

3. The prophet Ezekiel declares, "The soul who sins is the one who will die. The son will not share the guilt of the father, nor will the father share the guilt of the son."[11]

Make no mistake, God does not kill babies because their parents did something wrong. End of story.

Keeping these scriptures in mind should also help you view in a new light the death of King David and Bathsheba's first son.[12] After the prophet Nathan tells David the allegorical story of a rich man taking and killing the precious lamb of a poor man, David decrees that the culprit should not only die, but he should also experience a "fourfold" punishment.[13] Thus, the consequences for David's sins of adultery and murder came out of his own mouth, not out of the mouth of God. The untimely deaths of four of David's sons, beginning with his infant, underscores this point.[14] Yes, David and Bathsheba's baby became ill, and the Lord didn't answer David's prayer to heal his son, but based upon what we know of God's law and character, it is inappropriate to believe God killed the baby.

Neither did God kill your baby.

I make this assertion with confidence because of what I know about our Heavenly Father's character: He is a giver of life, and His mercy and lovingkindness endure forever.[15] When Jesus declared, "I have come that they may have life, and that more abundantly," He directly contrasted His nature with that of our enemy who comes to steal, kill, and destroy.[16] In fact, the Lord views the deaths of His children—including your baby—as a significant and sorrowful event that He does not take lightly: "Precious in the sight of the Lord is the death of His saints (godly ones)."[17] Let there be no doubt in your mind that the Lord considers your baby one of His godly ones.[18]

Not only does the Lord care *about* your children, He cares *for* them: "For the Lord delights in justice and does not abandon His saints (godly ones); They are preserved forever."[19] Therefore, you can have confidence in the fact that even though he or she is not currently visible to human eyes, your little one is now and forever in the Lord's care.

A Word in Due Season

If you are wondering what you should say to a person who is grieving infant loss, here is a list of some of the condolences that brought genuine comfort to the parents I interviewed.

"It's okay to grieve." Due to the stigma of miscarriage, too many of the parents I interviewed did not feel at liberty to grieve their loss, but several felt a sense of validation when told that it was okay to grieve. One mother viewed this as an opportunity to honor her baby's life.

"I am so very sorry you are walking through this pain." Parents found it comforting to have their loss acknowledged and their pain validated.[20]

"We share in your sorrow." Saying something like this lets grieving parents know that they are not alone in their suffering. We should never assume that those in mourning know we are also grieving their loss and are willing to be a part of their support system.

"I am praying for you." Knowing that others were lifting them in prayer gave strength and encouragement to parents. The effect of praying with those who are grieving shouldn't be underestimated: "You'll likely be able to ask God for help with a different level of faith than your hurting friend can muster....You can pray with a firm belief that creates stronger faith in others."[21]

"Baby." Using the word, "baby" and talking about the baby was important to the parents I interviewed. In addition, when others brought up the baby rather than avoiding the subject, parents felt gratitude and relief. Don't be afraid of hurting parents by bringing up the topic of the baby. Be more concerned about the pain that may be caused by avoiding the subject.[22]

Baby's name. If the baby was given a name, use Baby's name in conversations with the parents. One of the mothers I interviewed found it extremely comforting to hear others say her son's name:

> One of the biggest things for me is hearing someone else say my son's name or ask to know his name. It really means so much to me when my baby is remembered. It has inspired me to ask about and learn the names of other babies who have gone on before us. And to remember them too.

I want to single out one experience shared by a mother I interviewed because it is one of the most powerful expressions of consolation for a grieving parent I have heard. I pray you are equally blessed by these precious thoughts:

> A friend brought me flowers, and on the card she wrote, "These are not to remind you of life lost but of the beautiful eternal life that was created." Those words created an eternal perspective that became very real for me.

Through a single line of prose, this mother's sorrow was acknowledged, and the earthly life, loss, and eternal existence of her baby were remembered. This is consolation indeed.

Wisdom from Those Who Have Been Through It

Although I did not intentionally seek out Christians, all the parents I interviewed for this book were indeed Believers, and all but one of these parents explained that it was their faith in the Lord that helped them process their grief.[23] In fact, several stated that leaning upon their Heavenly Father as they mourned actually *strengthened* their faith.

Most of the parents with whom I spoke also expressed a desire to bless others who are enduring the pain of infant loss, so the following nuggets of wisdom were shared to bring comfort to grieving parents:

- "[J]ust because a bad thing happened, doesn't mean God is bad. God is Good all the time, and even though I didn't feel that at times, I knew *His* character well enough for it to be an anchor of hope during that time. We will experience circumstances that shake our very core, but it doesn't change who God is. There were times I couldn't trust my feelings. I could only rely on who I knew God to be."

- "Keep your eyes on the Lord and remember his goodness in the midst of anger, sadness, and confusion. Feel your feelings and be sad, but don't stay in that dark place for too long."

- "Remember that God's plan *is* perfect. Through the fire, we are refined. You may not understand it; you just have to trust Him. Also, remember that if you trust Christ with your life, you will have an eternity with your precious babies!"

- "True hope and joy are found in God alone!"

- "I have great comfort in God's perfect plan, even when it doesn't make sense to me. I think without trust in God, it most certainly would have been harder to move forward."

- "I will never forget my grandpa telling me, 'It [Baby's loss] makes heaven just a little bit more real doesn't it?' That has stuck with me ever since he said it. I think that it made my faith stronger and made me more eager to make sure I get to heaven one day. I think about heaven and Jesus a lot more because of it. I think of Jesus holding all the babies in heaven and how there's no pain or tears there, and how my baby has only known peace. Peace and Jesus. I think that is pretty amazing. Though my baby had a short life on earth, my baby has had a beautiful life."

- These scriptures were also found especially comforting to the parents I interviewed: Psalm 34:18; Psalm 71:20-21; Psalm 139:13; Psalm 147:3; Jeremiah 1:5; and 2 Corinthians 5:8.

The body of Christ is a community—a family. The Lord has called us to support one another physically, emotionally, and spiritually, and what better way to communicate love than to be there for one another in times of grief? Christians in the twenty-first century should not reserve the apostle Paul's encouragement to "comfort each other and edify one another" for conversations about theology and events that will take place at the Lord's return.[24] No, comfort for and edification of our sisters and brothers in Christ should be a lifestyle, and a large part of this life on earth is dealing with death.

You did not choose to become a part of the "society of grieving women," but you can use your experiences to alleviate the pain of others through your presence, your touch, your words, and your knowledge of the Lord's tools for grieving. If you notice a gap in infant loss support in your church or local area, find ways to fill that gap. By providing solace to others, you keep alive the memories of their children as well as your own.

1. 2 Cor. 1:3–5.

2. Capretto, "Empathy and Silence in Pastoral Care," 354.

3. Job 2:13.

4. It should be noted that very few people had been told about the pregnancies and early pregnancy losses of the 13% of mothers who did not receive hurtful "condolences."

5. Farrales et al., "What Bereaved Parents Want Health Care Providers to Know," 3.

6. Prov. 25:20, NLT.

7. Caldwell et al., "Women Pregnant after Previous Perinatal Loss"; Christiansen et al., "Parents Bereaved by Infant Death"; Shevlin et al., "Adult Attachment Styles."

8. Exod. 20:5. Additional references (Exodus 34:7, Numbers 14:18, and Deuteronomy 5:9) to God's declaration that He "visits the iniquity of the fathers on the children to the third and fourth generations" also come upon the heels of God's people's rejection of His sovereignty or of God's warnings about such rejection.

9. Deut. 24:16.

10. 2 Chron. 25:4.

11. Ezek. 18:20.

12. In chapters 11 and 12 of 2 Samuel, David forces Bathsheba into an adulterous relationship that results in a pregnancy. To cover his sin, David has Uriah (Bathsheba's husband) sent to the front lines of a battle to ensure his demise. After Uriah's death, David quickly marries Bathsheba to make it appear that the baby had been conceived in wedlock. The baby ultimately dies shortly after birth.

13. 2 Sam. 12:6.

14. 1) The son of David and Bathsheba (2 Sam. 12:14-18); 2), Amnon (2 Sam. 13:28-29); 3) Absalom (2 Sam. 18:14); and 4) Adonijah (1 Kings 2:25). Nathan's pronouncement that "the sword shall never depart from your house" was not necessarily a declaration that God was going to kill David's children, but it was rather a prophesy of what was to come as a result of David's failure to adequately teach his household how to heed God's laws (2 Sam. 12:10).

15. Pss. 23:6, 100:5, 106:1, 107:1, 118:1, 136:1-26.

16. John 10:10; Eph. 2:7; Exod. 34:6–7; Pss. 36:7, 86:5, 103:8–12, and 117:2; Titus 3:4–6.

17. Ps. 116:15, AMP.

18. Jesus made His feelings about children abundantly clear when He scolded His disciples for shooing away people who wanted Jesus to bless their infants: "Let the little children come to me, and do not hinder them, for the kingdom of God belongs to such as these" (Luke 18:15–16, NIV).

19. Ps. 37:28; Strong, *Strong's Exhaustive Concordance*, under "H8104, *shâmar*: to guard, attend to, preserve, save."

20. Wagner et al., "Fathers' Lived Experiences of Miscarriage."

21. Vroegop, *Dark Clouds, Deep Mercy*, 67.

22. Tracey and Murray, "Say My Baby's Name," 97. Tracey and Murray explained the necessity of talking openly about parents' loss: "[I]t is important to know that speaking about a baby who has died will not hurt parents—it is not speaking about the baby...that can cause the most pain."

23. I did not set out to collect only Christian perspectives; it simply worked out that the only people who responded to my inquiries were Believers.

24. 1 Thess. 5:11.

CHAPTER TWELVE

Moving Forward: Living with Scars and Hope

"I wait for the Lord, my soul waits,
And in His word I do hope."
PSALM 130:5

I HAVE A VERY large mirror on my bathroom wall, and as I toweled off following my morning shower not long ago, I performed an unconscious evaluation of my birthday suit. (I defy you, dear sister, to find a woman in North America who does not assess her body if presented with the opportunity, even if it is a simple, "Huh. Where did that bruise come from?")

Anyway, on this occasion, something caught my eye, and I paused to consider the various scars I had accumulated over the years. Tilting back my head, I stuck out my chin and began a mental inventory.

Yep, there is the ½-inch line under my chin that I've had as long as I can remember.

Next, I surveyed the broad, pale scar on my bicep that was left behind from a car accident in my early twenties. *Hmmm. Who knew an airbag could burn skin like that?* Leaning over, I peered at a two-inch line over my right ankle. *I wonder why that scar is still purple. It's been 25 years since that glass butterdish fell on the tile floor and sliced open my leg.*

Straightening back up, I poked at my abdomen. *Well, at least those three scars from my appendectomy aren't purple anymore. I wish the one over my bellybutton weren't so big.*

My running commentary stopped short as I looked back at the mirror and my eyes rested on the reflection of the largest scar. There, low on my pelvis, was a 5-inch horizontal line that had long ago faded to white—the only visible indication of the emergency surgery required when my fourth child went to heaven before birth.

Some scars are deeper than others.

With a sigh, I began to dress, pondering how these scars were rather like symbols on the roadmap of my life, representing events that had left their marks on me in more ways than one. Frankly, it seemed unfair that my body had preserved these physical reminders of sources of pain.

Closing my eyes, my thoughts turned to Jesus. *What about* Your *scars, Lord? Why do You even have any scars? When You were resurrected from the dead, why was Your body still scarred?*

At that point, I knew I needed to learn more about the Lord's scars because nothing with God is happenstance or coincidental. He has a reason for everything He does, and I was confident He was about to show me the purpose behind those scars.

Jesus Kept the Scars

It occurred to me that the only aspects of our Lord's physical appearance that are explicitly mentioned in the Gospels are His scars. Think about it: In no other way does the New Testament describe what Jesus looks like during His time on earth.

Everything we believe to be true about Christ's physical traits is conjecture founded upon Old Testament prophecies, educated guesses, and assumptions. For example, we assume Jesus had a medium-toned complexion, dark hair, and a beard because He was Jewish. Belief in the existence of Jesus's beard also comes from various descriptions of the Messiah's beard being plucked out during torture and humiliation.[1] Many Bible scholars also suggest that Jesus wasn't a classically handsome man because of what Isaiah prophesied about the coming Messiah: "He had no beauty or majesty to attract us to him, nothing in his appearance that we should desire him."[2] For many centuries, artists have attempted to capture the Lord's likeness on canvas and in marble, and as much as we may love some of these works of art, the fact is, the Lord's features in these images were based upon the artists' interpretations (often idealized and European) and not the Bible.

Despite human curiosity and desire for more information, the one and only thing our Heavenly Father has permitted us to know about Jesus's human appearance is that *He had scars.* In fact, there are only two places in the Bible that specifically refer to these scars: the Gospels of Luke and John. Within these accounts of Jesus's early appearances after His resurrection, we are told that the nails from the cross and the Roman centurion's spear left marks upon the Lord's body which remained after He rose from the dead. Even more significantly, it is through these accounts that we also find evidence for the reasons the Lord kept these scars.

Scars for Identification

The first indication of scarring on Jesus's body is found in Luke's Gospel when Jesus appears to the disciples following His resurrection and reveals His scars. Noticing His disciples' fear and uncertainty, Jesus asks them, "Why are you troubled? And why do doubts arise in your hearts?"[3] To reassure the disciples, Jesus shows them His scars: "'Look at my hands and my feet. It is I myself! Touch me and see; a ghost does not have flesh and bones, as you see I have.' When He had said this, He showed them His hands and feet."[4] Now, Luke doesn't blatantly say, "Jesus had scars on His hands and feet," but it appears Jesus was showing the disciples the places where the nails had pierced His body.

Charles Spurgeon, a nineteenth century British preacher, explained that Jesus revealed His scars to the disciples as a form of ID. Spurgeon explains that this was "to establish his identity, that he was the very same Jesus whom they had followed, whom at last they had deserted, whom they had beheld afar off crucified and slain, and whom they had carried to the tomb in the gloom of the evening."[5] Jesus knew His followers would need proof that He was who He said He was, and these scars were compelling evidence of the events that led to the death of their rabbi, Jesus of Nazareth—events His disciples had witnessed with their own eyes.

Scars for Thomas's Sake

The story of "doubting Thomas" in John 20 (the only place in the Bible where Jesus's scars are unequivocally mentioned, by the way) reveals Jesus also kept certain scars for one person: Thomas. Since he was absent when Jesus appeared to the other disciples, Thomas doesn't trust their story and declares he will "never believe" that Jesus is alive unless he can see and touch the "nail prints in His hands" and put his "hand into His side."[6]

Thomas's statements may seem rather macabre to some, but it sounds to me like the outburst of someone dealing with a broken heart. It's as if Thomas were saying, "I saw what the Romans did to Jesus, and I saw Him die, so forgive me, but your word is not enough to convince me. My pain is too deep, and my grief is too raw. I need concrete proof that the Lord is alive." It is also fascinating that of all the things the other disciples shared with him about their encounter with the Lord, Thomas focuses on Jesus's *scars*.

Thomas specifies that he needs to see with his own eyes the scars on Jesus's hands and side, and lo and behold, these are the very scars that remain. When Jesus returns to the disciples eight days after that initial appearance, He singles out Thomas, telling him, "Reach your finger here, and look at My hands; and reach your hand here, and put it into My side. Do not be unbelieving, but believing."[7] Jesus's words indicate there are marks on His hands and side, and these marks are substantial—deep enough for Thomas to insert his finger and his hand, but Thomas doesn't even touch the scars. Simply seeing them makes him exclaim, "My Lord and my God!"[8]

How marvelous to consider that Jesus would be willing to permanently scar Himself to meet the needs of one person. This idea isn't really that far-fetched, you know. Jesus Himself told the story of the Good Shepherd who was willing to leave the ninety-nine to seek out and attend to the needs of the one who was lost.[9] Thomas is lost in his grief, and because he wasn't there to see Jesus the first time he appeared to the disciples, Jesus seeks out Thomas by returning to show him the proof he'd requested. Jesus's attention to Thomas's needs aids his belief.

Christ's Scars: Ebenezers of Sacrificial Love

Christ's scars must have also revealed something more than His identity to the disciples, for the very wording Thomas uses to describe the marks left by the nails, *tupŏs*, is significant. This Greek word for "print" means "a stamp or scar; a shape that is a statue, style, or resemblance, specifically a sampler that is a model for imitation," so although the nail "prints" on Jesus's hands were evidence of His identity and divinity, these marks also gave His followers a "model for imitation."[10]

You see, the Romans intended the nails to hold Christ to the tree, but it was instead His love that held Him there, and the tupŏs left behind from this brutal death served as a type of memorial—an Ebenezer—of the sacrificial love required in ministry. Following Christ's example, each disciple would zealously spread the Good News of the Gospel to Jew and/or Gentile, with most giving their lives for this cause.

The Old Testament provides evidence that the Lord Himself views His scars as a type of Ebenezer as well: "I will not forget you; see, I have engraved you on the palms of My hands."[11] The connection between this statement and Christ's tupŏs is striking. Reading Isaiah 49:16 through the lens of the cross creates an image of the permanent engraving of our Messiah, the "precious cornerstone" and "sure foundation" for the Church, with marks that represent all the children He redeemed.[12]

Therefore, within the nail prints of His hands, Jesus sees your name and your image. Jesus does not keep His scars as a reminder of the painful death He endured. (He's omniscient; He doesn't need reminders.) No, He keeps the scars as symbols of all those for whom He died: human beings who would have no other means for relationship with Him but through the cross, the very source of those scars—humans who would be wounded and scarred themselves by the trials of life and who would need His help in living with those scars.

A New Perspective of Your Scars

Most human beings, including Christians, tend to regard scars in a negative light. Let's face it, humans see scars—be they physical, emotional, or spiritual—as evidence and constant reminders of damage, injury, a trial endured, and as imperfections or defects. (Consider how collectors view objects as more valuable if they are in "mint condition" or why people use filters or software to edit images of themselves for social media posts.) Scars don't seem to fit into human perspectives of beauty and perfection. However, this may be because humans do not often view scars through the corrective lens of the Lord's perspective. When we learn to recognize how the Lord views His own scars—Ebenezers of our redemption and victory over sin, death, and the grave—we may then take a different view of the scars from our own battles.

The Bible tells us our enemy comes "to steal, and to kill, and to destroy," and infant loss falls into all three of these categories.[13] Your child was stolen from you, his or her life was taken, and aspects of your own life were destroyed, including the plans and dreams you had for this child and your family. These are tragedies that cannot be denied, nor should they be. It is appropriate and expected that you will still weep and for ache for the child you cannot hold.

Make sure, however, you do not allow the enemy to take any more ground. Do not allow him to steal the Word from your heart. Do not allow him to steal the peace and comfort that the knowledge of God's character, promises, and faithfulness will provide. Remember and rehearse the Truth of the Word of God, for it is your sword of the Spirit—your weapon of warfare to combat the enemy of your peace.

I encourage you to avoid merely *enduring* trials and tribulations but to *overcome* them with the help of your Heavenly Father. If battle scars are left behind, learn to view those scars in a new light. You lived to tell the tale! This is not just the tale of what you went through, but it's also the tale of how the Lord brought you through it.

Let the perspective of one of the mothers I interviewed become a model for how to view the sorrow of miscarriage:

> We will experience trials. Pains. Anguish. Testing. Tribulation. Quiet deaths. A path with many unknowns yet to come. But the wonder of it all is that sorrows in the hand of the living God do not simply stay as they are. They hold the living water of the Holy Spirit's work in our life if we let Him in. *They become a home of remembrance of His kindness, His authority, and His strength* (emphasis added).

Rather than simply being the remembrance of your sorrow, learn to view your scars as a remembrance of the Lord's faithfulness.

Your scars are evidence that you are an overcomer, and you overcame because of your Father's great love for you. When the enemy comes against you, remember 1 John 4:4: "You are from God, little children, and have overcome because greater is He who is in you than he who is in the world." Meditate upon this promise and have confidence that your Savior enables you to overcome anything that is counter to Christ. When the enemy sets a snare of painful memories or difficult circumstances for you, know that Jesus encountered similar snares and overcame them because He is greater. He has the scars to prove it.

Faith is the Substance of Things Hoped For

I shall never view my scars the way I did when they were created. My scars have become for me a reminder—an Ebenezer—of my Heavenly Father's love and how He, in the middle of my storms of grief, has walked beside me and guided me through the process of mourning. My scars will remind me that I do not grieve like those who have no hope.

After all, the apostle Paul doesn't say in 1 Thessalonians 4:13-14 that Christians will not experience sorrow; he says we will not sorrow like people who have no hope.[14] This means we sorrow like people who *do* have hope. We have hope that death is not the end. We have hope in the fact that the world we see is not all there is. We have hope that in the spiritual realm we cannot see with human eyes, we will one day be reunited with our child(ren)—a reunion I look forward to with great anticipation as, I am sure, do you.

However, the hope of which Paul speaks is so much more than the promise of seeing our lost loved ones in the sweet by and by. No, the "hope" of which Paul speaks is an expectation, confidence, and faith in God.[15] We have hope in a God who is faithful and true. We have hope in a good, good God who provides for us in all of life's circumstances.

We can also have hope and confidence in the process of mourning available to Christians. We can cry out to Him, acknowledge the pain of the death of our children, make our complaints and requests known to Him, and remember and praise Him for His faithfulness with the assurance that the Lord's light will ultimately illuminate our current path of darkness.

Dear sister, your Heavenly Father's arms are opened wide as He waits to bring you the comfort and restoration you crave. When your soul feels as though it "melts from heaviness" and when you long to find "comfort in [your] affliction," go to the Word of God and let His Word give you strength and life.[16] Remember that nothing is so dark that it is hidden from God's sight. No event is so dark that it cannot be overcome by the love and glory of our Heavenly Father.

When you spend time in God's Word and in prayer, you are abiding in God's presence, and relationship has always been the desire of your Father's heart. Remember that Jesus, on the very night before He was crucified, exhorted the disciples to *abide in Him*.[17] Jesus knew His time on earth with them was short, so He emphasized the importance—the necessity—of dwelling and remaining in His presence and love: "As the Father loved Me, I also have loved you; abide in My love."[18] Abiding in the love of Christ while you are in mourning is where you will find the greatest hope and comfort:

> In a storm the tree puts down deeper roots into the soil; in a hurricane the inhabitants of the house stay inside and rejoice in its shelter. Through suffering the Father leads us to enter more deeply into the love of Christ....*In Christ*, the heart of the Father is revealed, and there can be no higher comfort than to rest in the Father's arms. *In Him* the fullness of the Divine Love is revealed, combined with the tenderness of a mother's compassion—and what can comfort like this?[19]

Only in God's presence can the hollowness left by your child's passing be filled. Only in the presence of the Lord can your broken heart be comforted and your wounds be healed. Only in the shadow of His wings will you get beauty in exchange for ashes, the oil of joy in exchange for mourning, and comfort and joy in exchange for sorrow. Only through the hope found in Christ will you experience restoration.[20]

> *The shaft of pain that shoots from gut to heart; the upward tilt of*
> *the chin and plaintive cry heavenward; the calm assurance in a*
> *loving Father who is trustworthy, faithful, and compassionate;*
> *the comfort of a peace the world can't comprehend—*
> *unexplainable, all-encompassing peace:*
> *This is hope.*

1. Isa. 50:6; Matt. 26:67; Matt. 27:26; Mark 14:65; Mark 15:19; Luke 22:63; John 18:22.

2. Isa. 53:2, NIV. The 53rd chapter of the book of Isaiah has long been considered a prophetic view of Israel's Messiah.

3. Luke 24:38.

4. Luke 24:39–40, NIV.

5. Spurgeon, "The Wounds of Jesus," para. 3.

6. John 20:25.

7. John 20:27.

8. John 20:28.

9. Matt. 18:12; Luke 15:4.

10. Strong, *Strong's Exhaustive Concordance*, under "G5179, *tupŏs*."

11. Isa. 49:15–16.

12. Isa. 28:16.

13. John 10:10.

14. 1 Thess. 4:13-14: "But I do not want you to be ignorant, brethren, concerning those who have fallen asleep, lest you sorrow as others who have no hope. For if we believe that Jesus died and rose again, even so God will bring with Him those who sleep in Jesus."

15. Strong, *Strong's Exhaustive Concordance*, under "G1680, *ĕlpis*: expectation, confidence."

16. Ps. 119:28, 50.

17. John 15:4.

18. John 15:9.

19. Murray, *The Essential Andrew Murray Collection*, 232, 234.

20. Ps. 16:11; Ps. 147:3; Isa. 61:3; Jer. 31:13; Ps. 30:11; Matt. 4:16; John 5:6.

Acknowledgments

When the Lord set before me the task of drafting a book on this challenging topic, He also provided me with the strength and support to accomplish it through the assistance of family, friends, and valuable new relationships.

I must first extend my great appreciation to each of the fifteen parents who responded to my questionnaire on miscarriage and infant loss. I know it was not easy to relive your experiences, and I want you to know that your feedback and words of advice were indispensable. I pray the Lord's special blessing on each of you as you continue to process your grief.

Thank you, Blair Parke for your talent and insight in editing my book. Your recommendations and kindness truly enhanced the final product. The Lord orchestrated our connection, and I am very grateful for it! Hannah Linder Designs was also instrumental in the creation of this wonderful book cover, and Hannah, I do so appreciate your creativity and patience in ensuring everything was just right.

To Virginia Wilson and Roger and Lennie Halvorson: You are more than parents. You are prayer warriors and amazing cheerleaders, and your support made a great impact on my writing process.

Thank you as well to my beta readers: family and friends who willingly took time out of their lives to read and offer advice. Victoria Slater, you were sent by God! I am obliged to you for your willingness to pore over so many chapters, and your honesty was invaluable. Deanna Stadley, thank you for your ideas, support, and continued boosts to my morale throughout this lengthy process.

Juliana Rose, I hope you realize how precious it has been to work through our mourning processes together and to address the losses that forever changed both our lives. Your ideas and encouragement as I produced the text before you have been a blessing.

Eric: I will be forever grateful for your steady, faithful, and loving support through the turbulency of the losses of two of our children. Thank you for being the strong husband and father you have always been and for your willingness to sacrifice our time together as I pounded away on my keyboard month after month. I am eager to see where the Lord takes us from here!

THE PREVALENCE OF MISCARRIAGE AND INFANT LOSS

The following statistics represent the instances of miscarriage in developed countries as of late 2025:

- Over 30% of pregnancies in the United States (US) end in miscarriage (up from the 10-20% reported in 2023).[1]

- "An estimated 23 million miscarriages occur every year worldwide, translating to 44 pregnancy losses each minute."[2]

- Worldwide, nearly 2 million babies are stillborn (die in utero after twenty-four weeks' gestation) each year.[3]

- A December 2025 report stated that the stillbirth rate in the US was 1 in 150 births (a higher rate than the 1 in 175 births reported by the CDC in 2021). What makes these losses even more concerning is that "no clinical risk factors were identified in 27.7% of all stillbirths and in 40.5% of stillbirths at 40 or greater weeks' gestation."[4]

- The later the pregnancy, the greater the risk of stillbirth: "[F]etal mortality was lowest at 29 weeks' gestation and highest at 41 or greater weeks' gestation."[5]

- Neonatal and post-neonatal mortality rates in the US increased by 3% and 4%, respectively, between 2021 and 2022.[6]

- Miscarriage and stillbirth rates at major community hospitals in California and Idaho have risen exponentially since 2020. For example, a nurse at one of these hospitals explained that prior to 2022, she had personally attended only one stillbirth per year. In 2023, she attended 17 stillbirths, and the numbers have continued to rise into 2025 (i.e., four stillbirths occurred in a two-week period in the summer of 2025).[7]

- Between 2018 and 2022, miscarriage rates in Lanarkshire, Scotland, increased 104.25%.[8]

- Neonatal deaths within 28 days of birth rose 166.66% in Lanarkshire, Scotland.[9]

- An Israeli study reported a 43% increase in expected miscarriage rates since 2021, and disturbingly, most of the miscarriages "occurred after gestational week 20 and nearly half occurred after gestational week 25."[10]

- Rates for miscarriage and infant demise in the US had experienced a steady *decline* between 1995 and 2021; however, these rates began to increase in the 2020s.[11]

---

1. Eighty percent of these occur prior to the twelfth week of pregnancy. "Miscarriage," *March of Dimes*, updated October 2024,
https://www.marchofdimes.org/find-support/topics/miscarriage-loss-grief/miscarriage#:~:text=Miscarriage%20is%20very%20common.,What%20is%20a%20threatened%20miscarriage%3F.

2. Quenby et al., "Miscarriage Matters," 1658.

3. "Why We Need to Talk About Losing a Baby," *World Health Organization*, updated 2025. https://www.who.int/news-room/spotlight/why-we-need-to-talk-about-losing-a-baby. WHO qualifies this statistic by noting that miscarriage and stillborn rates are likely even greater than this because mothers do not always inform their doctors when they experience infant loss.

4. Sullivan et al., "Stillbirths in the United States," 2035.

5. Sullivan et al., "Stillbirths in the United States," 2033.

6. Ely and Driscoll, "Infant Mortality in the United States."

7. The names of the nurses who provided this information and their places of employment (in two different states within the US) have been kept confidential.

8. Brownlie, *Obstetric Data for the Last 5 Years*. Miscarriage rates rose from 1,011 to 2,065, and neonatal deaths increased from to 16. It should be noted that Lanarkshire is one small county in Scotland, and although this county had no problem recording miscarriage and infant mortality rates, for some inexplicable reason, the NHS has not collected data on such deaths in the remainder of the UK. It is not unreasonable, however, to believe these numbers are representative of the entire UK. If this is the case, these statistics indicate that hundreds—if not thousands—more parents than in the two previous decades are grieving the loss of their unborn children in this first-world region.

9. Brownlie, *Obstetric Data for the Last 5 Years*.

10. Guetzkow et al., "Observed-to-Expected Fetal Losses," 1.

11. Ely and Driscoll, "Infant Mortality in the United States."

Miscarriage and Infant Loss Survey

(The following survey was issued to each of the fifteen parents who volunteered to participate in my research study.)

The following questions will be used for general analytical use. Your individual responses will not be given to any third party whatsoever; however, responses may be referenced in the published study. In addition, you will not be added to any mailing lists as a result of taking this survey. Proceeding with this survey implies that you understand and agree to the provisions in this disclaimer. Your identity will be kept confidential unless you provide your name in Question 1.

Please type your answers after each question. Take as much space as necessary. If you have experienced multiple miscarriages, please provide answers to questions 4-6 for each baby.

1. What is your name? (**To remain anonymous in the study, leave blank**.)

2. Race/ethnicity:

3. What is your current age?

4. What was your age at the time of miscarriage or infant loss?

5. Weeks of pregnancy at time of miscarriage or infant loss (i.e., baby died *in utero* prior to due date. *If your baby was born full-term, skip to question 6).*

6. If your baby was born full-term, how old was the baby when he/she passed away? (Express in weeks or days.)

7. Did your baby receive a birth and/or death certificate? If so, which type of certificate did you receive?

8. How did the receipt of the certificate(s) or the lack of receiving certificate(s) impact your perception of the baby and his/her loss?

9. How often do you think about your baby?

10. Did you receive any information on grief support from your physician, the hospital, or any outside sources? If so, what type(s) of support were discussed, and did you participate?

11. How did hospital or medical staff respond to your loss, and how did this impact you?

12. How did family and friends respond to your loss, and how did this impact you?

13. What expressions of condolence from others did you find helpful or comforting?

14. What statements from others or expressions of condolence did you find painful?

15. How have you addressed the loss of your baby, and what coping mechanisms did/do you find the most helpful (e.g., counseling, symbolic gestures, remembrances, etc.)?

16. How did the father of the baby cope with the loss?

17. The following questions relate to faith:

    a.   Would you describe yourself as a person of faith? (If no, skip to question 18.)

    b.   If so, how has your faith impacted your grief?

    c.   How has your grief impacted your faith?

    d.   What scriptures or maxims have aided your grieving process?

18. What would you like others to know about your loss?

19. What advice would you give other grieving mothers?

Present Thoughts and Feelings About Your Loss

Each of the items is a statement of thoughts and feelings which some people have concerning a loss such as yours. There are no right or wrong responses to these statements. For each item, circle the number which best indicates the extent to which you agree or disagree with it at the present time. (If you are working on this survey in MS Word, please highlight the number in yellow.) If you are not certain of your answer, select "Neither Agree nor Disagree." Please try to use this category only when you truly have no opinion.

Information in this questionnaire adapted from Lori J. Toedter, Judith N. Lasker, and Hettie J. E. M. Janssen's Perinatal Grief Scale: 33 Item Short Version in "International Comparison of Studies Using the Perinatal Grief Scale: A Decade of Research on Pregnancy Loss." *Death Studies* 25, no. 3 (2001): 205–228. doi:10.1080/074811801750073251.

Question	Strongly Disagree	Disagree	Neither Agree nor Disagree	Agree	Strongly Agree
1. I feel depressed.	1	2	3	4	5
2. I find it hard to get along with certain people.	1	2	3	4	5
3. I feel empty inside.	1	2	3	4	5
4. I can't keep up with my normal activities.	1	2	3	4	5
5. I feel a need to talk about the baby.	1	2	3	4	5
6. I am grieving for the baby.	1	2	3	4	5
7. I am frightened.	1	2	3	4	5
8. I take medicine for my nerves.	1	2	3	4	5
9. I very much miss the baby.	1	2	3	4	5
10. I feel I have adjusted well to the loss.	1	2	3	4	5
11. It is painful to recall memories of the loss.	1	2	3	4	5
12. I get upset when I think about the baby.	1	2	3	4	5
13. I cry when I think about him/her.	1	2	3	4	5
14. I feel guilty when I think about the baby.	1	2	3	4	5
15. I feel physically ill when I think about the baby.	1	2	3	4	5
16. I feel unprotected in a dangerous world since he/she died.	1	2	3	4	5
17. I try to laugh, but nothing seems funny anymore.	1	2	3	4	5

Question	Strongly Disagree	Disagree	Neither Agree nor Disagree	Agree	Strongly Agree
18. Time passes so slowly since the baby died.	1	2	3	4	5
19. The best part of me died with the baby.	1	2	3	4	5
20. I have let people down since the baby died.	1	2	3	4	5
21. I feel worthless since the baby died.	1	2	3	4	5
22. I blame myself for the baby's death.	1	2	3	4	5
23. I get angry with my friends and relative more than I should.	1	2	3	4	5
24. Sometimes I feel like I need a professional counselor to help me get my life back together again.	1	2	3	4	5
25. I feel as though I'm just existing and not really living since he/she died.	1	2	3	4	5
26. I feel so lonely since he/she died.	1	2	3	4	5
27. I feel somewhat apart and remote, even among friends.	1	2	3	4	5
28. It's safer not to love.	1	2	3	4	5
29. I find it difficult to make decisions since the baby died.	1	2	3	4	5
30. I worry about what my future will be like.	1	2	3	4	5
31. Being a bereaved parent means being a "Second-Class Citizen."	1	2	3	4	5
32. It feels great to be alive.	1	2	3	4	5

Appendix C:

MEDICAL TERMINOLOGY FOR BABIES, MISCARRIAGE, AND INFANT LOSS

Here are the most commonly used terms for babies, miscarriage, and infant loss as defined in Western medical dictionaries:

- ***Fetus/foetus***: "The human being in utero after the embryonic period and the beginning of the development of the major structural features, from the ninth week after fertilization until birth."[1]

- ***Fetal wastage or pregnancy wastage***: "A loss of a gestational product, either voluntary or involuntary, that occurs between the 20th [week] of pregnancy and the 28th day of life, a value known for epidemiological purposes, as 'total pregnancy wastage.'"[2]

- ***Perinatal loss***: "A death occurring within the period from 20 weeks gestation to 28 days after birth."[3]

- ***Miscarriage/Spontanous Abortion***: "[S]pontaneous loss of pregnancy before 24 weeks, formerly known as *spontaneous abortion*."[4]

- ***Stillbirth***: "Any child which has issued forth from its mother after the 24th week of pregnancy and which did not at any time after being completely expelled from its mother, breathe or show any other sign of life."[5]

- ***Zygote***: "The fertilized ovum before cleavage begins. It contains both male and female pronuclei."[6]

---

1. *Mosby's Dictionary of Medicine, Nursing & Health Professions*, "fetus/foetus," accessed July 30, 2024, http://ebookcentral.proquest.com/lib/nu/detail.action?docID=4615208.

2. *McGraw-Hill Concise Dictionary of Modern Medicine*, "fetal wastage," accessed July 30, 2024, https://medical-dictionary.thefreedictionary.com/fetal+wastage.

3. Kurz, "When Death Precedes Birth," 195.

4. *Oxford Concise Medical Dictionary*, "miscarriage," accessed October 3, 2023, https://www.oxfordreference.com/display/10.1093/acref/9780198836612.001.0001/acref-9780198836612-e-6309?rskey=ac6ZeR&result=4.

5. *Black's Medical Dictionary*, under "stillbirth," 625.

6. *Oxford Concise Medical Dictionary*, "zygote," accessed October 3, 2023. https://www.oxfordreference.com/display/10.1093/acref/9780198836612.001.0001/acref-9780198836612-e-11005?rskey=BhWTtf&result=1.

Appendix D:

PSALMS OF LAMENTATION

Scripture Reference	Psalmist	Initial Lament
Psalm 4:1	David	"Hear me when I call, O God of my righteousness! You have relieved me in my distress; Have mercy on me, and hear my prayer."
Psalm 7:1	David	"O LORD my God, in You I put my trust; Save me from all those who persecute me; And deliver me."
Psalm 10:1	Anonymous	"Why do you stand afar off, O Lord? / Why do you hide in times of trouble?"
Psalm 13:1	David	"How long, O Lord? Will you forget me forever? How long will You hide Your face from me?"
Psalm 22:1	David	"My God, My God, why have You forsaken Me? "Why are You so far from helping Me, And from the words of My groaning?"
Psalm 28:1	David	"To You I will cry, O Lord my Rock; Do not be silent to me, Lest, if You are silent to me, I become like those who go down to the pit."
Psalm 55:1-2	David	"Give ear to my prayer, O God, And do not hide Yourself from my supplication. Attend to me, and hear me; I am restless in my complaint, and moan noisily."
Psalm 61:1-2	David	"Hear my cry, O God; Attend to my prayer. From the end of the earth I will cry to You, When my heart is overwhelmed; Lead me to the rock that is higher than I."

Scripture Reference	Psalmist	Initial Lament
Psalm 69:1-3	David	"Save me, O God! For the waters have come up to *my* neck. I sink in deep mire, Where *there is* no standing; I have come into deep waters, Where the floods overflow me. I am weary with my crying; My throat is dry; My eyes fail while I wait for my God."
Psalm 70:1	David	"Make haste ,O God, to deliver me! Make haste to help me, O Lord!"
Psalm 77:1-3	Asaph	"I cried out to God with my voice— To God with my voice; And He gave ear to me. In the day of my trouble I sought the Lord; My hand was stretched out in the night without ceasing; My soul refused to be comforted. I remembered God, and was troubled; I complained, and my spirit was overwhelmed."
Psalm 83:1	Asaph	"Do not keep silent, O God! Do not hold Your peace, and do not be still, O God!"
Psalm 86:1-3	David	"Bow down Your ear, O Lord, hear me; For I am poor and needy. Preserve my life, for I am holy; You are my God; Save Your servant who trusts in You! Be merciful to me, O Lord, For I cry to You all day long."

Scripture Reference	Psalmist	Initial Lament
Psalm 88:1-3	Heman the Ezrahite	"Lord, God of my salvation, I have cried out day and night before You. Let my prayer come before You; Incline Your ear to my cry. For my soul is full of troubles, And my life draws near to the grave."
Psalm 102:1-2	Anonymous	"Hear my prayer, O Lord, And let my cry come to You. Do not hide Your face from me in the day of my trouble; Incline Your ear to me; In the day that I call, answer me speedily."
Psalm 141:1-2	David	"Lord, I cry out to You; Make haste to me! Give ear to my voice when I cry out to You. Let my prayer be set before You as incense, The lifting up of my hands as the evening sacrifice."
Psalm 143:1, 6	David	"Hear my prayer, O Lord, Give ear to my supplication! In Your faithfulness answer me, And in Your righteousness.... I stretch forth my hands to you; my soul thirsts after you, as a thirsty land."

THE GOSPEL IN A NUTSHELL

In Genesis 1:26, God said, "Let Us make man in Our image, according to Our likeness." The word for "image" is *tselem*, meaning "to shade; a resemblance; hence, a representative figure."[1] This word choice indicates that there is resemblance between God and human beings, and our shared attributes, both physical and spiritual, reveal our Lord's desire for relationship with us.[2] Unfortunately, Adam and Eve's rebellion against God introduced sin and death into the world, fracturing the relationship between humans and God. Sin cannot be in God's presence; therefore, humans could no longer commune with Him as before.

This did not prevent God's yearning for communion with His people, however. When He brought the Children of Israel out of Egypt, He ordered Moses to build a temple within their midst so that He could live among them: "I will dwell among the sons of Israel and will be their God. They shall know that I am the Lord their God who brought them out of the land of Egypt, that I might dwell among them; I am the Lord their God."[3] Despite their eventual entrance into the Promised Land (modern-day Israel), and despite warning after warning, God's Chosen People repeatedly forsook their relationship with Him over the next 1,000-1,500 years. The problem is humans are incapable of living up to God's Levitical Law, so the Israelites messed up again and again, preventing their ability to commune with God.

Therefore, the Lord had to do for humans what they could not do for themselves, and He sent His Son Jesus to repair the breach in the relationship between Himself and humankind. Insert here the most famous verse learned in Sunday school and emblazoned on posterboards at nationally televised football games: "For God so loved the world that He sent His only begotten Son, that whosoever believeth on Him should not perish but have everlasting life."[4] This was necessary because God had given man (Adam) free will and authority over a sinless and death-free earth, but since Adam used that free will to give away this authority, a human was required to regain it: "For since by man came death, by Man also came the resurrection of the dead. For as in Adam all die, even so in Christ, all shall be made alive."[5] Eternal life with God became possible for Jews and Gentiles alike because Jesus was sinless and took the sins of humankind on Himself: "For He made Him who know no sin to be sin for us, that we might become the righteousness of God in Him."[6]

Jesus died for every single person, taking our sins upon Himself so that we could again have communion with our Heavenly Father: "[K]nowing this, that our old man was crucified with Him, that the body of sin might be done away with, that we should no longer be slaves of sin....For the death that He died, He died to sin once for all."[7] With sin out of the way, humans may again spend as much time in God's presence as we desire. This is the good news brought to us by Jesus Christ!

---

1. Strong, *Strong's Exhaustive Concordance*, under "H6754, *tselem*."

2. Another important aspect of "tselem" reveals that the Lord created humans not just to reflect His image but also to be a representative of Himself on earth.

3. Exod. 29:45–46.

4. John 3:16.

5. 1 Cor. 15:21–22.

6. 2 Cor. 5:21.

7. Rom. 6:6, 10; cf., Heb. 9:28.

Appendix F:

THE NAMES OF GOD AND THEIR MEANINGS

Because he has set his love upon Me, therefore I will deliver him;
I will set him on high, because he has known My name.
PSALM 91:14

1. *Adonai*: Lord; Lord God; Master. Often used as verbal replacement for YHWH (Isa. 37:16).

2. *Attiq Yomin*: Ancient of Days (Dan. 7:9, 13, 22).

3. *Elohim*: God, Mighty Creator (Gen. 1:1).

4. *El Shaddi*: Almighty God (Gen. 17:1).

5. *El Elyon*: The Most High (Gen. 14:18–20).

6. *Jehovah Asah*: Lord our Maker (Ps. 95:6).

7. *Jehovah El Olam*: The Everlasting God (Gen. 21:33; Isa. 40:28).

8. *Jehovah Elohim*: Lord our God (Gen. 2:4; Ps. 84:11).

9. *Jehovah Jireh*: Jehovah will see; Jehovah see; the Lord will provide (Gen. 22:13–14).

10. *Jehovah M'Kaddesh*: God who sanctifies (Ex. 31:13).

11. *Jehovah Nissi*: Jehovah is my banner (Ex. 17:15).

12. *Yahweh Ra'ah/ Rohi*: The Lord My Shepherd (Ps. 23:1-3).

13. *Jehovah Rapha*: The Lord who heals (Ex. 15:26; 2 Kings 2:21, 20:8; Ps. 6:2; Ps. 41:3; Isa. 57:19).

14. *Jehovah Sabaoth*: Lord of Hosts (1 Sam. 1:3; 1 Sam. 17:45).

15. *Jehovah Shalom*: Jehovah is peace (Judg. 6:24).

16. *Jehovah Shammah*: The Lord is there (Ez. 48:35).

17. *Jehovah Tsidkenu*: The Lord our Righteousness (Jer. 23:6).

18. *Yahweh* (*YHWH* or *Jehovah*): God's sacred name. Typically translated as "Lord" or "Jehovah" (Ex. 3:14).[1]

---

1. Jeremiah, "The Names of God and Why They Matter"; Spangler, *Praying the Names of God*.

HEBREW AND GREEK WORDS TRANSLATED AS "PRAISE"

Hebrew Words for "Praise" with *Strong's Concordance* Numerical Designations and Definitions

1. *Bârak* (H1288): verb, "to kneel; to bless God." Used 331 times.

2. *Hâlal* (H1984): verb, "to shine; to glory or give light; to make a show; to boast; to rave; and to be clamorously foolish." Used 165 times (e.g., Judges 16:24; 2 Sam 22:4; Psalm 148:5; 1 Chron 23:30).

3. *Hillûl* (H1974): verb, "rejoicing; a celebration of thanksgiving for harvest." This word occurs only twice in the Old Testament: in Leviticus 19:24 to explain how the sacrifice of fruit is to be "holy to praise the Lord"; and in Judges 9:27 when Gaal and the men of Shechem were plotting to overthrow Abimelech and "made merry [hillûl]" with food and wine.

4. *Mahâlâl* (H4110): noun, "fame, praise." Used one time in Proverbs 27:21.

5. *Shâbach* (H7623): verb, "to address in a loud tone; commend; glory; triumph." Used 11 times.

6. *Shebach* (H7624): verb, "to adulate; to adore." Used 5 times.

7. *Tehillâh* (H8416): noun, "laudation, hymn, praise." Used 57 times.

8. *Tôdâh* (H8426): noun, "an extension of the hand (that is by implication an avowal or adoration); thanksgiving offering; confession." Used 32 times. Used as "praise" only four times: Psalm 42:4, Psalm 50:23, Jeremiah 17:26, and Jeremiah 33:11.

9. *Yâdâh* (H3034): verb, "to revere or worship with extended hands; cast; confess; give thanks." Used 114 times.

10. *Zâmar* (H2167): verb, "to touch the strings or part of a music instrument; to make music accompanied by voice; to celebrate in song and music." Used 45 times.

Greek Words for "Praise" with *Strong's Concordance* Numerical Designations and Definitions

1. *Aineō* (G134): verb, "to praise God." Used 10 times. For example, used in Luke 19: 37 to describe how the people praised Jesus as He was entering Jerusalem prior to His crucifixion. Also used in Revelation 19:5: "And a voice came out of the throne saying, 'Praise our God, all you His servants, and you that fear Him, both small and great.'"

2. *Ainesis* (G134): noun, "a thank offering." Used 1 time in Hebrews 13:15: "By Him therefore, let us offer the sacrifice of praise to God continually, that is, the fruit of our lips giving thanks to His name."

3. *Ainos* (G136): noun, "properly a story but used in the sense of praise

of God." Used 2 times.

4. *Aretē* (G703): noun, "Valor, excellence (intrinsic or attributed); praise virtue. Used 5 times.

5. *Doxa* (G1391): noun, "glory, honor, praise, worship." This word is used 168 times in the New Testament, but most of the time, it's translated as "glory." It's translated as "praise" only 3 times: In John 12:43 ("For they loved the praise [doxa] of men more than the praise [doxa] of God.") and in 1 Peter 4:11 when the apostle was encouraging the church to let all works of ministry be done so "that God in all things may be glorified through Jesus Christ, to whom be praise [doxa] and dominion forever and ever."

6. *Epaineō* (G1867): verb, "to praise, laud, commend." Used 6 times.

7. *Epainos* (G1868): noun, "laudation; a commendable thing." Used 11 times.

8. *Eulogeō* (G2127): verb, "to speak well of; to bless, thank, or invoke a benediction upon; bless praise." Used 44 times. For example, because of his doubt, the Lord made Zacharias mute, but immediately after naming John the Baptist, Zacharias could speak, and the first thing he did was praise (eulogeō) the Lord (Luke 1:64).

9. *Humneō* (G5214): verb, "to sing a religious ode; to celebrate God in song." Used 4 times (e.g., used to describe the Paul and Silas's songs of praise when they were in jail).[1]

---

1. Strong, *Strong's Exhaustive Concordance.*

A Deeper Dive into Praise

Kneeling in Praise

Physical forms of praise such as clapping, waving arms, dancing, or laying prostrate before the Lord are referred to throughout the Bible, but because these types of praise are usually translated into English as "praise," "bless," or "worship," modern readers may not always have a clear picture of the ways in which the Lord is being praised in any given circumstance. For instance, the word *bârak* has two meanings: "to kneel; by implication to bless God as an act of adoration."[1] Many of the biblical references to this word are translated as "bless" and indicate God's bestowal of favor upon humans (i.e., the Lord's blessing of Adam and Eve in the garden, Noah and his sons after the flood, and Abraham and Jacob when He promised to make them great nations).[2] However, there are dozens of examples in Scripture where "bârak" is used to describe humans' glorification and adoration of the Lord accompanied by kneeling, an outward sign of submission to God.

The bârak form of praise is evident within many of the psalms of David, including Psalm 31, a song of lamentation. It is believed that Psalm 31 was composed during one of Saul's numerous persecutions of David, so this song is an interesting study in how to grieve. There is an ebb and flow to this psalm; declarations of trust in the Lord are interwoven with cries of despair and pleas for the Lord's protection and mercy. Among David's complaints are that his eye, soul, belly, and life are "consumed with grief" and that he is "like a broken vessel."[3] David's misery is obviously great and founded upon real and present danger, but on the heels of his list of grievances, David heaps blessings upon the Lord:

> Blessed [bârak] be the Lord,
> For He has shown me His marvelous
> kindness in a strong city!
> For I said in my haste,
> "I am cut off from before Your eyes";
> Nevertheless You heard the voice of my supplications
> When I cried out to You.[4]

Notice David's vulnerability, honesty, and humility in these lines. His grief has caused physical and emotional harm, and David's very human (and relatable) reaction to such distress is to blurt out that the Lord has withdrawn from him and doesn't hear or see him.

The admirable thing about David is that he doesn't stay in this frame of mind, and he also recognizes how very wrong he was in accusing the Lord of things that weren't true. When David sings, "Bârak be the Lord," he is kneeling, showing his adoration of and submission to the Lord. David's choice of praise here is telling. It's as if he were saying, "Lord, I realize I was hasty in saying that you had cut off Yourself from me, and I want You to know that I appreciate the fact that You really do hear me and show me kindness despite my stupid words. I humble myself before the One who is the preserver of my soul."

Of the many lessons to be learned from this psalm is that God doesn't hold against us the things we say under duress as long as we remember who He is. Go ahead and vent your feelings and concerns, but don't leave things there. Recall to mind the goodness of your God, kneel before Him as an acknowledgement of

His sovereignty, and offer Him the praise He is due. When you humble yourself before the Lord, He will lift you up![5]

Lifting Hands in Praise

In addition to kneeling, raising hands before the Lord is another type of physical praise illustrated in Scripture that should be incorporated into your own worship. *Tôdâh* is the Hebrew word which is most often used to describe a praise offering or sacrifice, but this word also indicates a form of praise where one's hand is raised in open and earnest affirmation that the Lord is one's God; it is a way of acknowledging one's devotion to Him.[6] Studying tôdâh reminded me of the way a person raises his or her right hand prior to testifying in court or when taking an oath of office. This raising of the hand adds solemnity to an occasion, indicating that the person does not take this duty or obligation lightly. Keep in mind that Jewish law was explicit on the oath-taking process, so those who engaged in tôdâh praise would have understood its seriousness.[7] They would have viewed raising their hands during praise and sacrifice as an oath of service to the Lord.

Two additional intriguing points about tôdâh is that it is translated as "praise" only four times in the Old Testament, one of which is in Psalm 42, another lamentation.[8] Within this psalm, tôdâh praise is used to beautifully illustrate the path from despair to hope. The song begins with the psalmist's cry of distress to the Lord:

> As the deer pants for the water brooks,
> So pants my soul for You, O God.
> My soul thirsts for God, for the living God.
> When shall I come and appear before God?
> My tears have been my food day and night,
> While they continually say to me,
> "Where is your God?"[9]

We who have also experienced the throes of grief easily recognize the pain and despair this psalmist is enduring: around-the-clock tears, lack of appetite, and the sense that God is far away.

In addition to these symptoms, the psalmist also demonstrates the very common impulse to compare his current state of misery with former, happier days, but then there is a dramatic change of attitude. The psalmist wistfully remembers how he used to go with others to the temple "with the voice of joy and tôdâh," and this evokes a dramatic, almost instantaneous shift in his mindset: "Why are you cast down, O my soul? And why are you disquieted within me? Hope in God; for I shall yet praise [yâdâh] Him, The help of my countenance and my God."[10] These verses illustrate the quintessential volta, or about-face, in the psalmist's attitude. His comparison to "the good ol' days" reminds the songwriter of a time when he offered the sacrifice of praise to the Lord, and this memory of tôdâh triggers a remembrance of the goodness of his God. As a result, the psalmist refuses to let his mind take him down the path of negativity any longer. He tells himself not to dwell on the things that bring grief but to instead focus on the face of the Lord, declare that He is God, and make a conscious decision to hope in the Lord.

This is just another example of how the Lord provides for us in times of sorrow. Much like this psalmist, memories of praising the Lord in the past may lead to our ability to praise the Lord while in the midst of grief, and like this psalmist, remembering our past sacrifices of praise may guide us to other types of praise, such as *yâdâh*.

The yâdâh form of praise is a method of thanking and praising the Lord with expressive motions of the arms and hands. *Yâdâh* means "to revere or worship with extended hands; cast; confess; give thanks," creating the sense that one is hurling praises toward God.[11] Psalm 118 contains an example of yâdâh that is worth reviewing because this song of lament is atypical. Rather than following the usual lamentation formula of crying out to the Lord, complaining, requesting, and praising, Psalm 118 begins and ends with the same shout of praise: "O give thanks [yâdâh] to the Lord, for He is good! For His mercy endures forever."[12] The verses between these bookends of praise express the psalmist's distress at being surrounded by enemies, yet his stance of praise is intentional and defies natural inclination. His arms are extended, casting glory, honor, and praise upon his God. In the midst of—and in spite of—his suffering, yâdâh praise becomes the psalmist's first and last word regarding his current circumstances.

What this psalm demonstrates for those who are in mourning is the power of beginning and ending your lamentations with expressions of praise. You are not ignoring your circumstances or negating their severity. You are simply saying that their hold over you is nothing in comparison with the strength of your God. You can "cast your cares upon Him," and you can cast your praise upon Him "because He cares for you."[13] When you, like the author of Psalm 118, acknowledge that the Lord is on your side, you will also be able to declare with authority, "This is the day that the Lord has made; [I] will rejoice and be glad in it."[14]

That last lyric is not merely to be sung to an upbeat tempo on happy days (as is often the case in modern churches). These words should be declared as a reminder to ourselves to "[r]ejoice in the Lord always" because when we do, "the peace of God, which surpasses all understanding, will guard [our] hearts and minds through Christ Jesus."[15]

Verbal Expressions of Praise

Verbal expressions of praise, be they spoken or sung, occur more frequently in the Bible than the physical types, and because this is probably the type of praise you tend to use most often, it makes sense to examine the effects of this kind of praise. *Hâlal* is the Hebrew word for praise which means "to shine; to glory or give light; to make a show; to boast; to rave; and to be clamorously foolish."[16] I challenge you to find someone in the Bible who exhibited this type of praise more than David did throughout his lifetime and within his songs. Surprisingly, this demonstrative and boastful form of praise is also found within Psalm 22, another psalm of lamentation.

There are so many remarkable things to study in this prophetic song, but among these is the way Psalm 22 demonstrates how lamentation brings one into communion with the Lord God Almighty. After turning to the Lord and laying out a long list of heart-rending complaints, David makes the following declaration:

> You have answered Me.
> I will declare Your name to My brethren;
> In the midst of the assembly
> I will praise [hâlal] You."[17]

Even though David's circumstances have not yet changed, he acknowledges that God has heard his cries, has not hidden His face from him, and has answered his prayers. For these reasons, David uses hâlal praise to emphasize God's character and to honor and magnify Him. This is part of what makes hâlal different from other kinds of music. The singer/songwriter is not focused on self but on the Lord, and the result is an uninhibited, boastful, glorification of the Lord in front of God and everybody.

Another fascinating aspect of Psalm 22 is its first line is quoted by the Lord Jesus Christ during his crucifixion. Not long after He is hung on the cross, Jesus cries out, "My God, My God, why have You forsaken me?"[18] By shouting these words, Jesus directs those witnessing His crucifixion to Psalm 22, revealing that this song is talking about Him. The prophetic lyrics spoken on the cross not only declare Jesus's identification as the Messiah, but they also convey our Lord's humanness in feeling far away from His Heavenly Father during the most critical period of His life here on earth. Taking on the sins of the world forced a separation from His Father that Jesus had never experienced, and Christ's despair in that moment reveals the true tragedy of an existence apart from our God, something believers mercifully do not have to experience because of His sacrifice.

Because the elements of lamentation in Psalm 22 detail the suffering of David as well as of the Messiah, the psalm provides a roadmap to our restoration and reconciliation with God. After following the traditional process of lament, David is finally able to praise the Lord and to proclaim, "You have answered Me." Yes, these words are David's acknowledgment that God has heard his cries and that deliverance has been provided. However, Jesus's declaration on the cross also reveals that because the words of this psalm are prophetic of Him, the lyrics also apply to His followers. Therefore, the words, "You have answered Me," mean God answered Jesus's prayers, and God answers our prayers too.

Because of the redemptive work of our Messiah, when we are in the midst of lamentation, we can hold onto the hope that deliverance and restoration will come when we praise the Lord.

---

1. Strong, *Strong's Exhaustive Concordance*, under "H1288, *bârak*."

2. Gen. 1:22, 28; Gen. 5:2; Gen. 9:1; Gen. 12:2.

3. Ps. 31:9–10, 12.

4. Ps. 31:21–22.

5. 1 Pet. 5:6.

6. Strong, *Strong's Exhaustive Concordance*, under "H8426, *tôdâh*: an extension of the hand (by implication an avowal or adoration), a thanksgiving offering, or a confession."

7. "If a man makes a vow to the LORD or swears an oath to bind himself with a pledge, he must not break his word; he must do everything he has promised" (Num. 30:2).

8. Jer. 17:26; Jer. 33:11; Ps. 50:23; Ps. 42:5.

9. Ps. 42:1–3

10. Ps. 42:4–5.

11. Strong, *Strong's Exhaustive Concordance*, under "H3034, *yâdâh*."

12. Ps. 118:1, 29.

13. 1 Pet. 5:7.

14. Ps. 118:6, 24.

15. Phil. 4:5, 7.

16. *Strong's Exhaustive Concordance*, under "H1984, *hâlal*."

17. Ps. 22: 21–22.

18. Ps. 22:1; Matt. 27:46.

Appendix I:

"GREAT IS THY FAITHFULNESS" LYRICS

By Thomas O. Chisholm

Great is Thy faithfulness, O God my Father;
There is no shadow of turning with Thee;
Thou changest not, Thy compassions, they fail not;
As Thou hast been Thou forever wilt be.

Great is Thy faithfulness!
Great is Thy faithfulness!
Morning by morning new mercies I see:
All I have needed Thy hand hath provided—
Great is Thy faithfulness, Lord, unto me!

Summer and winter and springtime and harvest,
Sun, moon, and stars in their courses above
Join with all nature in manifold witness
To Thy great faithfulness, mercy, and love.

Pardon for sin and a peace that endureth,
Thine own dear presence to cheer and to guide,
Strength for today and bright hope for tomorrow—
Blessings all mine, with ten thousand beside!

CCRRE TEMPLATE FOR MOURNING

Use the following template as a guide for your mourning process and an encouragement to be intentional in your application of the principles of lamentation.

Steps Toward Hope and Restoration	Written Expressions
1. Acknowledge Baby's Life:	(Express acknowledgement here.)
2. Acknowledge Baby's Loss with Words:	(Express acknowledgement here.)
3. Acknowledge Baby's Loss with Deeds:	I will honor the memory of Baby by…
4. Call out to the Lord:	I am turning to the Lord in my grief by…
5. Complain to and Question the Lord:	I am hurting because… I have the following questions:
6. Request of the Lord:	I want the Lord to help me by…
7. Remember the Lord:	In the past, the Lord was faithful when…
8. Express Trust in and Praise to the Lord:	My favorite songs of praise and trust are…
9. Create an Ebenezer:	The memorial I will create/use to honor Baby is…

Bibliography

American College of Obstetricians and Gynecologists. "Facts Are Important: Understanding and Navigating Viability." Updated 2026. https://www.acog.org/advocacy/facts-are-important/understanding -and-navigating-viability.

American Psychological Association. "Thanatology." In *APA Dictionary of Psychology*. Edited by Gary R. VandenBos. American Psychological Association, 2015. https://research.ebsco.com/linkprocessor/plink?id=459d8cff-9 81c-3df5-82fd-640dc3c448ec.

Black's Medical Dictionary. "Dilatation and Curettage." Edited by Harvey Markovitch. Bloomsbury Publishing Plc, 2017; accessed October 29, 2025. https://ebookcentral.proquest.com/lib/nu/reader.action?docID=4 910872&c=UERG&ppg=200.

Black's Medical Dictionary. "SIDS." Edited by Harvey Markovitch. Bloomsbury Publishing Plc, 2017; accessed April 21, 2026. http://ebookcentral.pr oquest.com/lib/nu/detail.action?docID=4910872.

Black's Medical Dictionary. "Stillbirth." Edited by Harvey Markovitch. Bloomsbury Publishing Plc, 2017; accessed October 29, 2025. https://ebookcentral.proquest.com/lib/nu/reader.action?docID=4 910872&c=UERG&ppg=638.

Boss, Pauline. *Ambiguous Loss Learning to Live with Unresolved Grief*. Harvard University Press, 1999. https://doi.org/10.4159/9780674028586.

Brownlie, Linda. "Obstetric Data for the Last 5 Years" (Freedom of Information Request for NHS Lanarkshire, Scotland). What Do They Know? 2023. https://www.whatdotheyknow.com/request/obstetric_data_for_the_last_ 5_ye_8/response/2295660/attach/html/3/Maternity%20statistics%20Wilk ens%20March.doc.html.

Cacciatore, Joanne, Cybele Blood, and Sarah Kurker. "From 'Silent Birth' to Voices Heard: Volunteering, Meaning, and Posttraumatic Growth after Stillbirth." *Illness, Crisis, & Loss* 26, no. 1 (2018): 23–39. doi:10.1177/105 4137317740799.

Cacciatore, Joanne, John DeFrain, and Kara L. C. Jones. "When a Baby Dies: Ambiguity and Stillbirth." *Marriage & Family Review* 44, no. 4 (2008): 439–54. https://doi.org/10.1080/01494920802454017.

Caldwell, Julia Marysia, Pamela J. Meredith, Koa Whittingham, Jenny Ziviani, and Trish Wilson. "Women Pregnant after Previous Perinatal Loss: Relationships Between Adult Attachment, Shame, and Prenatal Psychological Outcomes." *Journal of Reproductive & Infant Psychology* 42, no. 4 (2024): 653–67. https://doi.org/10.1080/02646838.2023.2180142.

Capretto, Peter. "Empathy and Silence in Pastoral Care for Traumatic Grief and Loss." *Journal of Religion and Health* 54, no. 1 (2015): 339–57. doi:10.10 07/s10943-014-9904-5.

Carlson, Rose. "Ways to Commemorate October 15—Pregnancy and Infant Loss Remembrance Day." PLIDA: Pregnancy Loss and Infant Death Alliance. 2024. https://www.plida.org/october-is-pregnancy-and-infant-loss -awareness-month.

Cassidy, Paul Richard. "The Disenfranchisement of Perinatal Grief: How Silence, Silencing and Self-Censorship Complicate Bereavement (A Mixed Methods Study)." *Omega: Journal of Death & Dying* 88, no. 2 (2023): 709–31. doi:10.1177/00302228211050500.

Cha, Hyungmin, and Patricia A Thomas. "A Time of Healing: Can Social Engagement After Bereavement Reduce Trajectories of Depression After the Death of a Child?" *Journals of Gerontology Series B: Psychological Sciences & Social Sciences* 78, no. 10 (2023): 1717–26. doi:10.1093/geronb/gbad094.

Christiansen, Dorte M., Ask Elklit, and Miranda Olff. "Parents Bereaved by Infant Death: PTSD Symptoms up to 18 Years After the Loss." *General Hospital Psychiatry* 35, no. 6 (2013): 605–11. https://doi.org/10.1016/j.genhosppsych.2013.06.006.

Daniel, Terri. "Adding a New Dimension to Grief Counseling: Creative Personal Ritual as a Therapeutic Tool for Loss, Trauma and Transition." *Omega: Journal of Death & Dying* 87, no. 2 (2023): 363–76. doi:10.1177/00302228211019209.

Domogalla, Julie S., Janet McCord, and Rebecca Morse. "Rural Perinatal Loss: A Needs Assessment." *Omega: Journal of Death and Dying* 84, no. 4 (2022): 1045–60. https://doi.org/10.1177/0030222820926296.

Ely, Danielle M., and Anne K. Driscoll. "Infant Mortality in the United States, 2022: Data from the Period Linked Birth/Infant Death File." *National Vital Statistics Reports* 73, no. 5. (2024): 1–19. https://stacks.cdc.gov/view/cdc/157006.

Farrales, Lynn L., Joanne Cacciatore, Christine Jonas-Simpson, Shafik Dharamsi, Jaime Ascher, and Michael C. Klein. "What Bereaved Parents Want Health Care Providers to Know When Their Babies Are Stillborn: A Community-Based Participatory Study." *BMC Psychology* 8, no. 1 (2020): 1–8. https://link.gale.com/apps/doc/A616409412/HWRC?u=nu_main&sid=bookmark-HWRC&xid=bfc5a496.

Farren, Jessica, Maria Jalmbrant, Nora Falconieri, et al. "Posttraumatic Stress, Anxiety and Depression Following Miscarriage and Ectopic Pregnancy: A Multicenter, Prospective, Cohort Study." *American Journal of Obstetrics and Gynecology* 222, no. 4 (2020): 367.e1–e22. doi:10.1016/j.ajog.2019.10.102.

Figueredo-Borda, Natalie, Mirliana Ramírez-Pereira, Pedro Gaudiano, Cecilia Cracco, and Beatriz Ramos. "Experiences of Miscarriage: The Voice of Parents and Health Professionals." *Omega: Journal of Death & Dying* 89, no. 2 (2024): 777–94. doi:10.1177/00302228221085188.

Fleming, Katherine, and Emma Roth. *When Fetuses Gain Personhood: Understanding the Impact on IVF, Contraception, Medical Treatment, Criminal Law, Child Support, and Beyond.* Pregnancy Justice, 2022. https://issuelab.org/resources/42820/42820.pdf#.

Gabriel, Charles H. *The Singers and Their Songs: Sketches of Living Gospel Hymn Writers.* Rodeheaver, 1916. https://catalog.hathitrust.org/Record/100194527.

Gruber, Mayer Irwin, and Louis Isaac Rabinowitz. "Oils." In *Encyclopaedia Judaica.* 2nd ed. Vol. 15. Edited by Michael Berenbaum and Fred Skolnik. Macmillan Reference USA, 2007. https://go.gale.com/ps/retrieve.do?tabID=T003&resultListType=RESULT_LIST&searchResultsType=SingleTab&retrievalId=96df6b0d-10f5-4723-ace8-c7de3487a90e&hitCount=40&searchType=AdvancedSearchForm¤tPosition=9&docId=GALE%7CCX2587515052&docType=Topic+overview&sort=Relevance&contentSegment=&prodId=GVRL&pageNum=1&contentSet=GALE%7CCX2587515052&searchId=R2&userGroupName=nu_main&inPS=true https://link.gale.com/apps/doc/CX2587515052/GVRL?u=nu_main&sid=bookmark-GVRL&xid=b717e416.

Guetzkow, Josh, Tal Patalon, Sivan Gazit, et al. "Observed-to-Expected Fetal Losses Following mRNA COVID-19 Vaccination in Early Pregnancy." *medRXiv: The Preprint Server for Health Sciences*, ahead of print, June 2025. https://doi.org/10.1101/2025.06.18.25329352.

Higginbottom, Ryan. "Biblical Lament: What Is It and How to Do It." Open the Bible with Pastor Colin Smith. June 13, 2022. https://opentheBible.org/article/biblical-lament-what-it-is-and-how-to-do-it/.

Howlett, Sandra. "Creating Meaningful Memorials After the Death of Child." New Song Center for Grieving Children. Accessed October 15, 2025. http s://www.hov.org/media/1083/ns_5543_creating_meaningful_mem.pdf.

Idaho Statutes Title 32, Domestic Relations § 32-102. Unborn Child as Existing Person. 2025. https://law.justia.com/codes/idaho/title-32/chapter-1/secti on-32-102/.

Jaffe, Janet, and Martha O. Diamond. "Grieving a Reproductive Loss." In *Reproductive Trauma: Psychotherapy with Infertility and Pregnancy Loss Clients*. American Psychological Association, 2011. doi:10.1037/12347-0 05.

Jeremiah, David. "The Names of God and Why They Matter." DavidJeremia h.org. Accessed September 16, 2024. https://www.davidjeremiah.org/knowgod/the-names-of-god?nbt=nb%3A adwords%3Ax%3A21288420231%3A%3A&nb_adtype=&nb_kwd=&nb_ ti=&nb_mi=&nb_pc=&nb_pi=&nb_ppi=&nb_placement=&nb_li_ms= &nb_lp_ms=&nb_fii=&nb_ap=&nb_mt=&gclid=Cj0KCQjwrp-3BhDg ARIsAEWJ6Sym3KgsAsIIP7ZbVKxF0TZ6falLImVTHWyHCpiWnWB pSQRB0CrZpVkaAi79EALw_wcB.

Jones, Kerry. "Parental Identity in Narratives of Grief Following Perinatal Death." *Grief Matters: The Australian Journal of Grief & Bereavement* 17, no. 2 (2014): 38–42. https://search.ebscohost.com/login.aspx?direct=true &AuthType=sso&db=a9h&AN=97910633&site=ehost-live.

Juhasz, Esther. "Tzitzit" In *Encyclopedia of Jewish Folklore and Traditions*. Routledge, 2013. https://research.ebsco.com/linkprocessor/plink?id=c92 722b9-4fb1-3e1e-8794-812f82c6bf66.

Kübler-Ross, Elisabeth. *On Death and Dying*. Taylor & Francis, 1973. https://research.ebsco.com/c/yi2or4/ebook-viewer/pdf/3s2uny4ncf?locati on=https%25253A%25252F%25252Fresearch.ebsco.com%25252Fc%2525 2Fyi2or4%25252Fsearch%25252Fdetails%25252F3s2uny4ncf%25253Freq uest-context%25253Dplink%252526db%25253Dnlebk.

Kurz, Maria Renée. "When Death Precedes Birth: The Embodied Experiences of Women with a History of Miscarriage or Stillbirth—A Phenomenological Study Using Artistic Inquiry." *American Journal of Dance Therapy* 42, no. 2 (2020): 194–222. doi:10.1007/s10465-020-09340-9.

Lang, Ariella, Andrea R. Fleiszer, Fabie Duhamel, Wendy Sword, Kathleen R. Gilbert, and Serena Corsini-Munt. "Perinatal Loss and Parental Grief: The Challenge of Ambiguity and Disenfranchised Grief." *Omega* 63, no 2 (2011): 183–96. doi:10.2190/OM.63.2.e.

LaValley, Kristen. *Even if He Doesn't: What We Believe about God When Life Doesn't Make Sense.* Tyndale Momentum, 2024.

Lawrence, Natan. "Abiding Under the Shadow of His Wings." Hoshana Rabba Blog: Midrash with Natan Lawrence. Updated June 18, 2016. https://hoshanarabbah.org/blog/2016/06/18/under-the-shadow-of-his-wings/.

LeDuff III, Lawrence D., Wanda T. Bradshaw, and Stephanie M. Blake. "Transitional Objects to Facilitate Grieving Following Perinatal Loss." *Advances in Neonatal Care* 17, no. 5 (2017): 347–53. doi:10.1097/ANC.0000000000000429.

Ling, John R. *When Does Human Life Begin? Christian Thinking and Contemporary Opposition.* The Christian Institute, 2017. https://www.christian.org.uk/wp-content/uploads/when-does-human-life-begin.pdf.

March of Dimes. "Miscarriage." Updated October 2024. https://www.marchofdimes.org/find-support/topics/miscarriage-loss-grief/miscarriage#:~:text=Miscarriage%20is%20very%20common.,What%20is%20a%20threatened%20miscarriage%3F.

Mcgee, Katie, Morgan E. PettyJohn, and Kami L. Gallus. "Ambiguous Loss: A Phenomenological Exploration of Women Seeking Support Following Miscarriage." *Journal of Loss & Trauma* 23, no. 6 (2018): 516–30. doi:10.1080/15325024.2018.1484625.

McLelland, Kristi. *Jesus and Women: In the First Century and Now.* Lifeway Press, 2019.

Middlemiss, Aimee Louise. *Invisible Labours: The Reproductive Politics of Second Trimester Pregnancy Loss in England.* 1st ed. Vol. 54. Berghahn Books, 2024. https://search.ebscohost.com/login.aspx?direct=true&AuthType=sso&db=nlebk&AN=3736945&site=ehost-live.

Mitima-Verloop, Huibertha B., Trudy T. M. Mooren, and Paul A. Boelen. "Facilitating Grief: An Exploration of the Function of Funerals and Rituals in Relation to Grief Reactions." *Death Studies* 45, no. 9 (2021): 735–45. doi:10.1080/07481187.2019.1686090.

Murray, Andrew. *The Essential Andrew Murray Collection: Humility; Abiding in Christ; Living a Prayerful Life.* Bethany House, 2021.

The New Scofield Study Bible. Edited by C. I. Scofield. Thomas Nelson Publishers, 1989.

Oxford English Dictionary. 7th ed. Edited by Maurice Waite. Oxford University Press, 2012.

Park, Crystal L. "Religion as a Meaning-Making Framework in Coping with Life Stress." *Journal of Social Issues* 61, no. 4 (2005): 707–729. doi:10.1111/j.1540-4560.2005.00428.x.

Quenby, Siobhan, Ioannis D Gallos, Rima K Dhillon-Smith, et al. "Miscarriage Matters: The Epidemiological, Physical, Psychological, and Economic Costs of Early Pregnancy Loss." *The Lancet* 397, no. 10285 (2021): 1658–67. doi:10.1016/S0140-6736(21)00682-6.

Reagan, Ronald. Proclamation No. 5890. 53 Fed. Reg. 208, Oct. 25, 1988. https: https://archives.federalregister.gov/issue_slice/1988/10/27/43413-43426.pdf.

Robinson, O. F. *Penal Practice and Penal Policy in Ancient Rome.* Routledge, 2007. https://research.ebsco.com/linkprocessor/plink?id=34cbe64e-6c94-3e34-a1a9-e4ab6cfb527a.

Rothschild, Jennifer. "How Long, O Lord?" In *When You Pray: A Study of Six Prayers in the Bible.* Edited by Becky Loyd. Lifeway Press, 2023.

Shevlin, Mark, David Boyda, Ask Elklit, and Siobhan Murphy. "Adult Attachment Styles and the Psychological Response to Infant Bereavement." *European Journal of Psychotraumatology* 5, (2014): 1–9. https://doi.org/10.3402/ejpt.v5.23295.

Shreffler, Karina M., Patricia Wonch Hill, and Joanne Cacciatore. "Exploring the Increased Odds of Divorce Following Miscarriage or Stillbirth." *Journal of Divorce & Remarriage* 53, no. 2 (2012): 91–107, https://doi.org/10.1080/10502556.2012.651963.

Smith, L. K., J. Dickens, R. Bender Atik, C. Bevan, J. Fisher, and L. Hinton. "Parents' Experiences of Care Following the Loss of a Baby at the Margins Between Miscarriage, Stillbirth and Neonatal Death: A UK Qualitative Study." *BJOG: An International Journal of Obstetrics and Gynecology* 127, no. 7 (2020): 868–74. doi:10.1111/1471-0528.16113.

Spangler, Ann. *Praying the Names of God.* Zondervan, 2004.

Spurgeon, Charles. "The Wounds of Jesus" (Sermon, January 30, 1859). The Spurgeon Center for Biblical Preaching at Midwestern Seminary. 2017. https://www.spurgeon.org/resource-library/sermons/the-wounds-of-jesus/#flipbook/.

Strong, James. *Strong's Exhaustive Concordance, Complete and Unabridged.* Baker Book House, 1983.

Sullivan, Haley K., Anna D. Sinaiko, Kathe Fox, Joanne C. Armstrong, Mark A. Clapp, and Jessica L. Cohen. "Stillbirths in the United States." *JAMA: Journal of the American Medical Association* 334, no. 22 (2025): 2033–35. https://doi.org/10.1001/jama.2025.17392.

Toedter, Lori J., Judith N. Lasker, and Hettie J. E. M. Janssen. "International Comparison of Studies Using the Perinatal Grief Scale: A Decade of Research on Pregnancy Loss." *Death Studies* 25, no. 3 (2001): 205–228. doi:10.1080/074811801750073251.

Tracey, Anne, and Marie Murray. "Say My Baby's Name." In *Stillbirth and Miscarriage, a Life-changing Loss.* Cork University Press, 2022. https://research.ebsco.com/linkprocessor/plink?id=459ba12a-2799-3859-8323-5e5b46fd7963.

Uber, Marjorie, Renata Robl, Kerstin T. Abagge, et al. "Hematohidrosis: Insights in the Pathophysiology." *International Journal of Dermatology* 54, no. 12 (2015): e542–43. doi:10.1111/ijd.12932.

VandenBos, Gary R., and American Psychological Association. "Thanatology." In *APA Dictionary of Psychology*. American Psychological Association, 2015. https://research.ebsco.com/linkprocessor/plink?id=459d8cff-981c-3df5-82fd-640dc3c448ec

Vroegop, Mark. *Dark Clouds, Deep Mercy: Discovering the Grace of Lament.* Crossway, 2019.

Wagner, Nathaniel J., Colin T. Vaughn, and Victor E. Tuazon. "Fathers' Lived Experiences of Miscarriage." *The Family Journal* 26, no. 2 (2018): 193–99. doi:10.1177/1066480718770154.

Watson, Jo, Anne Simmonds, Michelle La Fontaine, and Megan E. Fockler. "Pregnancy and Infant Loss: A Survey of Families' Experiences in Ontario Canada." *BMC Pregnancy and Childbirth* 19, no. 1 (2019): 1–14. doi:10.1186/s12884-019-2270-2.

Wigoder, Geoffrey, Fred Skolnik, and Shmuel Himelstein, eds. "Tallit." In *The New Encyclopedia of Judaism*, 2nd ed. New York University Press, 2002. https://search.credoreference.com/articles/Qm9va0FydGljbGU6M TA5NjczOQ==?aid=102577.</div>.

Wommack, Andrew. *The Effects of Praise*. Harrison House, 2012.

World Health Organization. "Why We Need to Talk About Losing a Baby." Updated 2025. https://www.who.int/news-room/spotlight/why-we-need -to-talk-about-losing-a-baby.

Yeivin, Ze'ev and Louis Isaac Rabinowitz. "Yoke." In *Encyclopaedia Judaica*. 2nd ed. Vol. 21. Edited by Michael Berenbaum and Fred Skolnik. Macmillan Reference USA, 2007. https://link.gale.com/apps/doc/CX2587521286/ GVRL?u=nu_main&sid=bookmark-GVRL&xid=68ac031b.

Zhou, Ningning, Yicheng Wei, Clare Killikelly, et al. "The Relationship Between Social Acknowledgment and Prolonged Grief Symptoms: A Multiple Mediation Effect of Beliefs about the Goodness and Controllability of Grief-Related Emotions." *European Journal of Psychotraumatology* 14, no. 2 (2023): 1–12. doi:10.1080/20008066.2023.2220633.

About the Author

Cheri Y. Halvorson has six children (two of whom went to be with the Lord before they were born) and six grandchildren, one of whom also resides in heaven. As an educator with a Master of Arts degree in English Literature from California State University, Fresno, Cheri has taught combinations of English, academic writing, and humanities (medieval-Renaissance Period) at colleges and universities since 2014. Cheri resides in North Idaho with Eric, her husband of thirty-eight years, and loves studying and teaching the Bible, recognizing that there is always more to learn within God's living Word.

www.ingramcontent.com/pod-product-compliance
Lightning Source LLC
Chambersburg PA
CBHW061422160726
47995CB00003B/713